He Lives

Other books by the author

BOLD TO SAY
YOUR MORALE
LIFE OUT THERE

He Lives

by

AUSTIN PARDUE
The Bishop of Pittsburgh

MOREHOUSE-GORHAM CO.
New York
1946

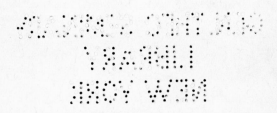

To my son Peter
with whom I discussed many
of the points in this book.
While this dedication does
not commit him to full agreement, it does express my
appreciation.

CHAPTERS

CONTENTS

INTRODUCTION

IN THE early days of World War II, a remarkable coincidence occurred in Buffalo, N. Y. at 2:00 A.M. on the same day.

At approximately that hour a door-bell rang long and loud. The mother was the first to wake. Immediately her thought was of her son. "Do you suppose he could be home on furlough?" She hurried into a kimono and sped downstairs to the door. There he stood—large, strong, beaming, and radiant! They fell into each other's arms and then ran upstairs to wake the family. The reunion was completed around the dining-room table with a full meal at three-thirty A.M. The whole family stayed up all night rejoicing and talking.

Another front door-bell rang about the same hour that morning at the home of a widow. She had raised her son by doing housework. He was a good boy, faithful to his Church, and in High School became the outstanding model-airplane-builder in the city. Now he was a gunnery sergeant in the Air Corps. The door-bell rang, and this mother also wakened with a similar hope that it might be he. She too hurried into a kimono and flew downstairs to answer the bell. She opened the door and there stood a Western Union Telegraph delivery boy. She took the telegram and numbly dragged herself upstairs. She turned on the light in the living-room and sat in his chair and began to read that fatal line, "We regret to inform you that your son was killed this afternoon." She, too, was up all night.

A few days after that morning I was invited to the home of the first boy for dinner to celebrate his return. On that same day I held the burial service for the second boy who had been killed in Texas on a routine bomber run.

The triumph of the Christian religion is this: The mother of each boy held the same general hope and aspiration. Each wanted to see her son grow up to be fine and strong and worthy. One is living, the other is dead. Yet, the Christian faith teaches that death makes little difference. The aspirations of both mothers can be fulfilled. The son who is to fulfil his purpose upon earth has exactly the same job as the one who is to fulfil his purpose in Paradise; namely, that of soul and character growth. There is no death and there is no separation under the doctrine of the Communion of Saints. The second mother will see her son face to face, and, judging from the fine start that he had when he was here on earth, she will see her hopes and aspirations and ideals fulfilled.

During World War II, I found it difficult to obtain modern publications written in plain terms on the subject of "Immortality and the Communion of Saints." I felt there was a need to preach and teach on this great theme of unity between the Churches, Militant, Expectant, and Triumphant. Since most of the popular material available seemed to miss this emphasis, I decided to publish short articles in the cathedral weekly bulletin. These articles met with an immediate response, and are the basis of this book. When I became Bishop of the Diocese of Pittsburgh, weekly celebrations of the Holy Communion were held at the Cathedral for the families of every boy or girl who was killed in our forces. The bereaved families likewise needed and wanted instruction. Thus, this book comes out of my pastoral experience.

In a very real sense, this is a testimony to my own religious experience. I refer to "my faith" and "my religion" only in the sense of that which I know through practice. The book is based on the teachings of the historic Church and the Book of Common Prayer. The teachings which we inherit on the subject of "Immortality" from these sources must constantly be made new in terms of personal experience. They should be inwardly digested through prayer, meditation, and reason. In this sense, these statements are a part of "my religion."

Much of this subject must be based upon faith rather than on scientific proof. Even the scientists themselves are forced to accept much of their data on faith. Suppose a boy starts out to study medicine. After college he arrives at medical school and has a vast amount of scientific data to assimilate. He goes from class to class and emerges with bulging notebooks full of thoughts taught to him dogmatically and taken by him on faith. If he had to stop and rationally prove and examine all of the information that is poured into him, he could not graduate in a lifetime. So he accepts the bulk of his material on the faith and experience of those who teach him. Proof, for the most part, will come only by later years of medical practice.

If there has been a death in your family, or in your close circle of immediate friends, you will be better off if you accept much on faith and prove it by devotional practice. It will be necessary for you to assume that our Lord and the teachings of His Church are true, and thereby you will go ahead and practice the religion of the Prayer Book until it becomes an experience which gives you definite knowledge. You will then experience the joy of the doctrine of the Communion of Saints.

AUSTIN PARDUE
Bishop of Pittsburgh

Chapter I

PANORAMA

THERE is a beautiful oriental rug covering the floor of an enormous baronial hall. In the middle of the rug, a caterpillar is laboriously working his belly-wise way toward some destination of which he seems not too sure. Progress is slow and confused because this particular species of caterpillar is strangely susceptible to the influence of color. He is crawling through the midst of a seemingly endless and intricate design of many colors. His travel is, of necessity, so close to the design that he cannot possibly see its contour, point, or purpose. Confusion conquers perspective. Life to him is a series of surprises, many of which are unpleasant. First, he finds himself in the midst of a portion of cobalt blue, and he responds with a spell of feeling blue; next he is in the yellow, which makes him feel bright and well again; crawling on, he finds himself in a patch of brown, in which he feels achy and tired all over; now he turns to red in the design and he fairly burns up with emotional uncontrol, which so overstimulates his adrenal glands that his confusion soon turns to biliousness. He wanders on into a stretch of green, and so life continues—a meaningless combination of confusions. In the midst of life, he is in pleasure, pain, sadness, joy, sickness, and, finally, in despair.

Suddenly he is struck by a great idea; he decides to assemble a convention of the best minds in the caterpillar intellectual world. He sends out the call and from all four corners of his rug come the mighty of brain and political influence. Certainly with so many good heads assembled for the cause of better understanding, great things will emerge. They meet, pass resolutions, debate, appoint commissions, and adjourn as do those at almost every other convention. So they all go back, each to his own particular kind of confused pleasure-pain existence. They know not one whit more now than when they started out, except that all of them are in the same predicament.

Life goes on for our friend out in the middle of the vast rug: he proceeds with heavy heart, an irritable disposition, a hyperacid stomach, and complete disillusionment. After long nights of insomnia, he finally drops off into a deep sleep—for how long he does not know. When he awakens he is suddenly aware of a change in his life; something has happened. What is it? He sits up, takes a good look at himself, and wonder of wonders, he has become a butterfly. A beautiful yellow colleague swoops down over him and calls "Come on up here and have a look." Our friend slowly spreads his wings. What power he feels! He takes off, uncertain at first, and then with mighty pulls he feels himself being propelled up and up. As he peers down upon the rug, he sees that all of those painful colors which he kept getting into, without knowing why, are part of a great design. Now he realizes that, when he had been in the midst of the rug, he could do nothing but blunder from one event to another without reason or understanding. No wonder life on the rug was hell. In a flash, life becomes clear to him and his problems are reduced to a new understanding. From above, he can see where he has been; the past is full of meaning; he can see where he was just a second ago and where he is now. But what is even greater, he can see into the future. From where he is, the past, present, and future are all one great whole. What a wonderful way to live, to be able to see where you are heading and to know why. So back he goes to the rug. Now he moves with confidence and joy. He knows that he has wings and can rise above his problems. So can everyone who is born of the Spirit.

Chapter II

THE TRIUMPH OF DEATH?

THE greatest tragedy of modern religion is the loss of a driving faith in the indestructibility of the human soul. Present-day Christians still observe Easter, recite ancient creeds, and sing Resurrection hymns, but collectively little do they feel of the motivating force that should cause them to face the sins of this materialistic world with a fearless hope. The constant impact of the worship of things, the corresponding flattery of the human ego which lifts reason above divine revelation, and the successful revival of the cult of the Golden Calf, have given force to the leadership of Lucifer and have almost won the day for the triumph of belief in death. Yet, there is a remnant of believers rallying the forces of eternity for a counter-attack which will yet rout the propagandists of disbelief.

The social implications of the doctrine of eternal death are greater than we realize. Many modern college students have emerged from a pagan classroom fully propagandized to sneer at Christian doctrine as a mythical fabrication created from psychological escape complexes. With catch phrases of a liberalism so broad it believes in little or nothing ringing in their impressionable ears, the faith of our fathers that gave America her strong start has been thoroughly debunked. Eventually, the man on the street also becomes a skeptic, not by processes of reason, but from the general debunking infiltration. The total result is that no longer do we believe in life but in death. Since death is our end, a future judgment is of no consequence. Thus, if there is to be no day of reckoning, if no bills need be paid, if no debts must be settled—well, then let's get away with what we can while we may.

Morality without God is like guns without bullets. International ethics without personal responsibility can never save us from the atomic bomb. Only Christ's love in men's hearts can do that. Let's not be foolish, wishful thinkers. If there is to be a great new day in American thinking, there must be a revival in the basic Christian belief in God's judgment of man and the survival of human personality. Jesus, the resurrected Saviour of mankind, must again become the assurance of everlasting life. Otherwise, to the millions of bereaved we can offer no other consolation than a sad shaking of the head and our embarrassed mumblings of sympathy. Is there anything worse than to see a person who does not truly believe in immortality trying to offer comfort to a bereaved friend? But, praise God, the Church has the truth about immortality; we have a way of communication, and we are beginning again to teach our truth to the spiritually starved whose sons are not dead but alive.

Everything in the future depends on this basic doctrine. It is far more important for world peace, social security, and racial compatibility, than pacts, political promises, and intellectual explanations of humanistic theories. Because, in dealing with the subject of life after death we are talking about the deepest of motivations. If we really believe that we are put here to prepare for eternity and that our acts will be judged, we will probably decide to start living in the Kingdom now. Otherwise, why worry about ideals? This is blunt but it is human and realistic. The ideal is to worship without reward, but that we will learn in a Christian post-graduate course. Most of us are sinful and selfish and we are, at this stage, motivated by rewards and punishments. Some day, God willing, we will love God without recompense. That is our spiritual aim. For now, teach the fundamentals.

Chapter III

THE CHURCH HAS THE ANSWER

IT USUALLY takes a war or some other tragedy to make most of us question the quasi-scientific intellectuals who have told us that all life dies with the death of the body. When thousands of telegrams begin to reach out across a nation with the fatal opening line, "We regret to inform you," and when the personal effects are sent home —we then turn to the altar to hear "Therefore with Angels and Archangels, and with all the company of heaven" and say, "That is true. Yes, that includes him, for he too is now a part of the company of heaven." When we return to the faith of the Church we can rise confidently to our feet and say the Creed. With it there comes a new lift as we repeat "I believe . . . . . in the Communion of Saints . . . . . the Resurrection of the body; and the Life everlasting. Amen."

Many debunking intellectuals and destructive liberals have little to offer those families whose sons have not returned, or whose closest earthly companions have died. They can be graciously sympathetic; they can recite memories of how fine he was; and they can offer jokes to try to make us forget, but that is of little tangible aid to broken hearts. Yet, there is something to be offered; there is a concrete belief, a definite and constructive strength to be received. The Church of the ages has a doctrine of indestructible Catholic heritage that belongs to us all; a doctrine that will unite us with the dead in a living union now.

Belief in the Communion of Saints is one of the richest gifts bequeathed to man by the Church of antiquity. Too few know its great meaning and fewer still understand its unifying application whereby the world of the unseen enters the world of the visible. Roman Catholic abuses in the form of indulgences and the crass belief that souls could be bought out of purgatory did more to cause the Protestant Reformation than any other one factor. One of the tragedies of human history was this prostitution of the truth of the Resurrection, this shocking advantage taken by those who betrayed the trust of the Holy Church at the expense of the bereaved who remain on earth.

On the other hand, the reformers, instead of reforming the abuses, denied a priceless part of the faith. This was not by malicious intent. It was rather a blind, human mistake springing out of boiling prejudice, which resulted in a tragic negation. The negation made the faith so sterile of inter-world communion that prayer no longer bridged the great gulf now fixed. The Reformation often brought about an isolationism between the two worlds of the seen and the unseen. In an attempt to correct these abuses, many of the reformers taught that the souls of the dead were either in heaven or hell, and, since it was impossible for the living to contact either place, they might just as well wait and mourn until the general resurrection. The great Protestant Reformation, with all of its nobility, left the new Church in the same predicament a boy is in who goes to the barber, falls asleep in the chair, and instead of getting a "trim" wakes up nearly scalped.

Around Pittsburgh, you can dig coal in almost any backyard. As a matter of fact, there is a strip-mine about a block and a half from my house. The parable is told of a baby boy, about two years of age, who strayed from the kitchen to play in the backyard which was virtually a soft coal bed. When the mother found the child, he was black from head to foot. She rushed him into the kitchen, took an old galvanized tub, filled it with water, and bathed him vigorously. When she finished giving him the bath, the water was so black that the good mother, who loathed dirt, picked up the galvanized tub and rushed for the back door throwing out the entire contents, including the baby. The desire to get the baby clean resulted in the disposing of the child along with the dirty bath water. Much of the Reformation was done in that mood.

Yet, the Church, in spite of the many miserable failures and sins of her adherents, has managed to retain the undaunted faith of the ancient Christians. To this day she holds the priceless truth and still stands ready to offer to a bereaved America the living faith that Christ intended be taught to all people. Thus, with full knowledge of the unworthiness of her adherents, and with humble confession of their past sins, she teaches that part of Christianity known as the Doctrine of the Communion of Saints. The doctrine of the Communion of Saints does not deal with the concept of a mere memorial for the departed. A memorial relates us to a past event which is now extinct in all but the memory. The practical application of our belief has to do with an active association with the departed who are now living vital lives apart from the flesh. By this, we mean that the Church can bring us into an intimate relationship with them now, today.

We have a concrete faith which is seldom taught by the general run of denominational Churches. Yet, fundamentally, almost all of the denominations do accept the Apostles' Creed which stands for the doctrine of the Communion of Saints. So, in reality, the basis for a full faith is intrinsic in most Churches, but their ministers have simply neglected to teach it. The Book of Common Prayer amplifies and enlarges upon this doctrine in many ways, yet the majority of its adherents are without clear conviction or practice on the subject. With the faith of the Communion of Saints, we should not compromise. If we as a Church begin to believe and practice that doctrine, we will become aware of a greater Christian fellowship between the seen and the unseen.

Chapter IV

EVIDENCE AT THE EMPTY TOMB

I AM the resurrection and the life, saith the Lord: he that believeth in me, though he were dead, yet shall he live: and whosoever liveth and believeth in me, shall never die." With that sentence begins the triumphal entry of the casket. It is the first sentence of the Burial Office from the Book of Common Prayer.

Christianity rests upon the above premise. If it is fact, it is the greatest event that ever happened in history; it offers the greatest hope to all who cherish the idea of a life of continual growth with those whom we have loved; it makes primary the surrender of everything to Christ the King; it threatens the one who would deliberately deny Him with being cast out into outer darkness.

Yet, if the premise is false, Christianity is the greatest hoax that has ever been perpetrated upon the human race. It makes Christ Himself a character who is unparalleled in the history of the deliberate lie; it makes the millions of Christians throughout history, their sufferings and their sacrifices, the most devilishly deceived block of hopeless humanity that was ever known. These words sound like an extravagant exaggeration, but they are not. Christ either rose from the dead, or He did not, and any silly compromise between the two positions is not Christianity. Just how that event took place, and with what Resurrected Body He presented Himself, we do not know. How can we know, and why should we know? We probably wouldn't understand if we did know, and in addition we would forfeit the benefits of faith if we demanded that we understand. I am willing to rest the case on the fact that there are certain mysteries in things of the spirit which cannot be rationalized any more than my love for my wife and children can be reduced to a test-tube analysis. The Resurrection of Christ must be accepted if we would be Christians.

Apologetic theorizers do not help substantiate Christianity by concocting various interpretations of the Resurrection in order to please the skeptics. Christianity rests thoroughly on the fact that Jesus must have risen on the third day. It is the only reason to account for the miraculous change of attitude on the part of the scattered band of defeated and bedraggled Apostles. If, when the women visited the tomb on Easter morning, it was not found to be empty, then they must have lied. Having watched their brave vigil at the foot of the cross on Good Friday, one would hardly have cause to believe that they would bear false witness three days later. They were not that kind of women. Furthermore, the lie, had it been one, would have been quickly contradicted by a visit to the tomb, for the evidence would be obvious.

There has been a weak argument called the "theft

theory." This is an ancient argument and can be found in the 28th chapter of St. Matthew's Gospel, the 12th verse. When the Chief Priests "were assembled with the elders, and had taken counsel, they gave large money unto the soldiers, saying: Say ye, His disciples came by night, and stole him away while we slept. And if this come to the governor's ears, we will persuade him, and secure you. So they took the money, and did as they were taught: and this saying is commonly reported among the Jews until this day." This accusation is obviously contrary to the tested character of the Apostles. How anybody could read their post-Resurrection lives and then believe that they could do such a thing is inconceivable. To believe that they could steal the body and then build their new unconquerable spirit upon the theft is preposterous. Had they stolen away the corpse, certainly they would have been intelligent enough to know that the less said about the empty tomb the better.

There are many other ancient and popular explanations which still could not account for the victorious change in the Apostles. There is the futile notion that the women met a young man who their vivid imaginations thought was an angel, and that inadvertently they were directed to the wrong grave. Also, there has been the thought that our Lord swooned on Good Friday afternoon and that three days later, under the influence of the cool air of the tomb and the aromatic spices used in His embalmment, He revived. In all the accounts of the Crucifixion there is no ground for not believing that our Lord was dead after the blood and water had come from His side. It has also been said that the post-Resurrection appearances of our Lord were due to the overwrought feelings of the Disciples. This reduces the phenomena of Christianity to an origin based on psychological abnormalities. Who, in his right mind, could believe that the mighty army of Christians, martyrs, and confessors, could thunder down through the ages, borne on a hallucination?

The oldest report of the Resurrection of Jesus Christ, after His crucifixion, is found in St. Paul's first Epistle to the Corinthians 15:1. It has a concise air of conviction as it states, "Moreover, brethren, I declare unto you the gospel which I preached unto you, which also ye have received, and wherein ye stand; By which also ye are saved, if ye keep in memory what I preached unto you, unless ye have believed in vain. For I delivered unto you first of all that which I also received, how that Christ died for our sins according to the scriptures; And that he was buried, and that he rose again the third day according to the scriptures: And that he was seen of Cephas, then of the twelve: After that, he was seen of above five hundred brethren at once; of whom the greater part remain unto this present, but some are fallen asleep. After that, he was seen of James; then of all the apostles. And last of all he was seen of me also, as of one born out of due time."

This was written in the early fifties of the first century, probably twenty-five years after the actual event when a great many eye-witnesses were still alive. Accounts of the Resurrection also appear in the four Gospels. St. Paul has many other references, and certainly the Resurrection was the center of his teaching. There are other references in the New Testament, and on the whole, testimony comes from eye-witnesses. In St. Matthew's Gospel we have two Resurrection appearances; in St. Luke there are three; in St. Mark there are at least five; and in St. John's Gospel, three. St. Paul's account, although amazingly economical in its use of words, is the fullest account and it is interesting to note that he records six appearances after the Resurrection, including the one to himself.

St. Paul bases his whole faith upon the truth of the Resurrection. "If Christ be not risen, then is our preaching vain." . . . If we believe that Jesus died and rose again, even so "they also which are fallen asleep in Christ" will God bring with Him. There is no question where he stands. He goes so far as to assume that already his readers are convinced of the fact, and he is therefore able to build his argument upon it.

It is interesting to note what a challenge the empty tomb was to the Roman authorities. All they needed to do was to produce the body to disprove this seemingly wild resurrection statement. It was necessary only to bring in the barest clue of the remains to crush the enthusiasms of the small group of despised followers. The authorities failed utterly. After all of the debunking of the Resurrection has taken place, the final and most difficult hurdle is to disparage the witness of the "five hundred brethren at once." Mary Magdalene might have been emotional; St. Thomas might have been phlegmatic; St. Peter might have been unstable; St. Paul might have been epileptic; but not all of the five hundred could have been hypnotized. The Acts of the Apostles concludes, "He showed himself alive by many infallible proofs."

The Apostles stake everything on their convictions of the Resurrection. The very qualification for admission to the Apostolate was to be "a witness of the Resurrection." St. Peter declares that God raised up Jesus from the dead, and clinches it by saying "We did eat and drink with Him." St. Paul says that He was "seen for many days." These witnesses were convinced and satisfied that the risen body was real and that it had been identified. Furthermore, they were sure that it had been endowed with new power, raised to a new plane of existence.

There is no doubt but that something of colossal moment occurred. When you look at the seeming total failure of the mission of Christ as He hangs on the cross; when you follow that apparent defeat to the desertion of His followers, surely it would not seem that this great Christian Church throughout the world could stand a day as a witness to such a hopeless ending. Peter, who attested to the lie that he never knew Jesus, would not in a comparatively few hours be racing about the countryside shouting "He is risen." Something happened. It just isn't sensible to think that this powerful force of men and women could walk triumphantly to their deaths on a false premise. The origin and powerful growth of the Christian Church had its beginning in the Resurrection. There is no other possible answer.

Besides the direct evidence of the Christian Church itself, we have the added witness given us by the existence of the Lord's Day. Most of the early Christians had been Jews and their sacred day was Saturday, the Sabbath, the seventh day of the week. The importance and sacredness of this day is attested to by Jewish Rabbinical writings. Yet those same Jews changed that all-important day from the seventh to the first day of the week. Why? Obviously, because Jesus rose from the dead on the first day and from then on the significance was so powerful that they made the change. Had it been otherwise, the Apostles would have set Friday, the anniversary of our Lord's death, as the great day. However, Sunday was chosen and has changed the calendar habits of the whole world. Each first day of the week is a minor Easter and is constant testimony to the fact of the Resurrection.

The Holy Communion, or the Holy Eucharist, is also a testimony. It not only commemorates our Lord's death but also "His mighty Resurrection and glorious Ascension." It is a feast of joy, which was established from the very earliest days of Christianity. It is and has been the principal service of the Church throughout the ages.

Chapter V

SCIENCE AND THE INVISIBLE

IN THESE days when the cyclotron can transmute matter into energy, when the secret of the sun is discovered and applied to the disintegration of the atom of uranium, when alcohol is made into tires, when coal becomes the basis for stockings, and when the electric eye, television, and radar make visible those things which for ages have been invisible, it is not difficult for one to believe that the Son of God could rise from the tomb of death.

We can't seem to believe in the power of the invisible because it isn't objectively proved to our satisfaction. Yet, who understands the scientific miracles within the reach of our finger-tips? Edison said himself that he did not pretend to understand what electricity is. Even household electronic mysteries we take for granted. True, we may know the mechanism, but not one thing of the energy that operates it. You walk into a house, you push a button, and a miracle in electricity occurs as the lights flash on. You move to a comfortable chair, switch on the radio, and invisible forces are selected out of the atmosphere within the room and audibly produced through the loud speaker. You go out into the kitchen and there you find the ice-box containing the miracle of refrigeration. You go to the dentist's office, place a piece of celluloid in your jaw, and in broad daylight and without so much as a flash, the miracle of X-ray has occurred. Your boy flies a B-29 and by means of radar, which he likewise takes for granted, he is able to detect the enemy and save the crew. Yet, who understands these miracles all about us? Do you know anyone who refuses their benefits because they cannot fathom their secrets? Why are we so willing to take the mysteries of a material world completely on faith but rule out spiritual claims wholesale?

Harvard's famed professor of astronomy, Harlow Shapley, has produced a book entitled *A Treasury of Science* and in it some astounding things have been said about the atom. One atom of uranium holds within it 175,000,000 electronic volts. Each atom is a solar system in itself, with a sun or central nucleus, wherein is contained this unbelievable power. And how big do you suppose an atom might be? Well, it is invisible in the first place, even to the most powerful of the modern microscopes. It is stated in this book that it would take the entire population of the world 10,000 years to count the atoms in one drop of water, and in addition to that, each individual counter would have to be reduced to one billionth of an inch in order to see an atom. Yet the atom has been split, the energy has been released, the new day of the world is dawning, and the unbelievable occurs and changes everything. Yet the atom is invisible. So also are the forces of the Spirit which faith claims are the laws behind the atom.

The atom was broken down by an instrument called the cyclotron, developed by Dr. E. O. Lawrence. Thus, the atomic bomb is able to destroy matter, and turn matter into energy. Christ was able to heal. He was able to turn water into wine, and, as a matter of fact, there was nothing that He seemed unable to do in either the spiritual or the physical world. And that goes for today. Dr. Alexis Carrel, the famous Nobel Prize winner in surgery, Commander of the Legion of Honor, said, "Prayer is an invisible emanation, the most powerful form of energy one can generate . . . as demonstrable on the human mind and body as that of the secreting glands. A habit of sincere prayer will noticeably alter your life. Within the depths of consciousness a flame kindles . . . prayer is a force as real as terrestrial gravity. Prayer is like radium; a force of luminous, self-generating energy. Prayer links up with the inexhaustible motive power that spins the earth. If prayer is released and used in the lives of common men and women, if the spirit declares its aim clearly and boldly, there is yet hope that our prayers for a better world will be answered."*

In 1919, Lord Rutherford made a great advance toward splitting the atom. He discovered the nature of alpha rays emitted by radium. These rays were able to transmute elements. He sent them crashing into the nuclei of nitrogen, and oxygen resulted. Later Dr. Lawrence came into the scene with his now famous cyclotron. He proposed to

* "Prayer Is Power," *The Reader's Digest*, March 1941.

take a weaker force and split it up by degrees until finally, when unleashed, it would overpower the atom's defense. He sent streams of deuterons crashing into the nuclei of other atoms in an increasingly destructive barrage. Soon Dr. Lawrence was changing familiar elements like platinum into other elements like gold. Thirty-four different elements were subjected to bombardment with his eighty-five-ton cyclotron, and all of them underwent a transformation. Isn't it quite probable that something similar happened at various times in our Lord's ministry? Why Bible critics continue to insist on rationalizing all the supernatural out of the miracles, when scientists can transmute matter into energy and energy into matter, is amazing to say the least. How much easier to accept the Resurrection now that the cyclotron is making possible the same kind of things that our Lord performed here on earth.

New Testament evidence often differs in detail which only confirms the belief in the sincerity of the writers. If all stories were identical, it would seem strange, but since they were individually told from the point of view of each person's own convictions, honesty rings from every one of the sacred records. Should an accident happen on any busy city corner, and if a few minutes later each of the witnesses was asked to write the details of the accident, no two accounts would be identical but all would agree on the great fundamentals of what occurred. These Gospel and Epistle accounts of the Resurrection which agree whole-heartedly on the fact but occasionally differ on the details, are in many ways the results of the same kind of situation.

There is much evidence of the actual Resurrection of the physical body. Our Lord's body had been dead for only some forty hours, and, if God wanted to, He certainly could have revived the physical body. Furthermore, we are told that our Lord invited His apostles to feel His wounds; also, He ate with them, and the marks of the crucifixion were manifest.

There was an equally convincing belief that our Lord's body at the Resurrection was transmuted into some kind of spiritual body. St. John, himself, seems to believe this. There are accounts of how He passed through closed doors, which had been locked, and of how He made Himself visible or invisible, and all of this I can easily believe. As a matter of fact, He might have been able to do these things even when He was in His physical body. There was a time when He was face to face with a destructive mob who would have done away with Him but "He passed through the midst of them" and apparently went on His way untouched. St. John and St. Peter were convinced of the Resurrection when they looked into the empty tomb and saw that Jesus had passed out of His graveclothes without even disturbing them. Personally, I believe that He might have appeared long enough in His physical body, with its wounds, to convince His followers of the reality of His Resurrection. I can believe either one or both, it makes no difference. In a sense I do believe both, for He could have experienced the Resurrection any way He so desired. Naturally, we do not know the exact details at this time but some day we probably will. In the meantime, I am sure that the Resurrection occurred, and that upon it rests the whole faith of the Christian Church. In it rests our hope.

Chapter VI

HOW MUCH ARE YOU WORTH?

ONCE I visited a museum which exhibited the chemical ingredients composing the human body. There in a case were bottles containing ordinary water, lime, iron, calcium, and the various other bodily components. What interested me most was the astonishing statement that all of these elements were worth about ninety-eight cents. So some of us may be worth, as a top price, a dollar and a half and others as little as fifty cents. Is that all? Then why are some insured for a million dollars? Certainly those inexpensive chemicals in the bottles cannot bring such a bonanza to underwriters. Obviously, it is the mysterious thing called life or human personality which brings the worth of a policy into the million dollar class. If the one you love the most is nothing but a group of mere chemicals, which can be purchased for a dollar or so in any drug store, then it would be far more sensible to purchase the ingredients of the human flesh, keep them in bottles, and spend our affections in this most economical fashion. Such is the logical conclusion for those who do not believe in the immortal soul.

Let's carry the illogical cult of the worship of the physical body one step further. Suppose that the greatest of scientific laboratories could create a human body from the various chemicals in the museum bottles. Suppose that these scientists had the genius to make a human eye with all of its wondrous complications of nerves, muscles, and cells; suppose that they could create the exact replica of the human brain, the stomach, the respiratory system, and our glandular mechanisms. All right, let us imagine that they can do it. Here is the exact facsimile, a triumph of biochemistry stretched out upon a laboratory slab. Then what? Where is life, where is spirit, where is love, where is personality, where is character, where is sacrifice, where is kindness? Can the scientists make the real man? Obviously man is made in two parts; that which is of the flesh, and that which is of the spirit. The flesh passes; the spirit never dies but is called to a life of growth, development, and great adventure.

A person's real worth can be determined only by the qualities developed within his soul which have eternal values. What are those values of lasting significance? In historic Christian language they are known first under the head of the Theological Virtues, which are faith, hope, and charity; secondly, as the Cardinal Virtues, which are justice, temperance, fortitude, and prudence. We might also add the Gifts of the Spirit, composed of Holy Fear, Godliness, Wisdom, Understanding, Knowledge, Counsel, and Ghostly Strength. Study these gifts and virtues in such a book as *The Elements of the Spiritual Life,** by F. P. Harton, and see what kind of permanent stuff you are made of.

* S.P.C.K., publishers.

Chapter VII

AS THEY REALLY ARE

THE first step in building up a sense of companionship with those who have died or been killed is to
try to see them as God made them. We need to develop
enough imagination to visualize beyond the limitations
of flesh and bones. God made man a sort of a sacrament
in himself; he has a temporary outward and visible appearance and an inward, spiritual, and invisible (to the
physical eye) reality. St. Paul says that you have two
bodies; the one is perishable, corruptible, temporary, and
material. True, it is a wonderful instrument while it
lasts; it is a miracle of divine engineering. It is built to
serve the other body, the permanent and spiritual one,
for a short time, for the purpose of teaching a specific
lesson, but then it is to be cast off. So the second body,
after the death of the physical body, is to be raised in
glory, in incorruption and in sure and certain victory over
physical death.

I do not know of all the reasons God places us in a
physical body and world for a period of time, but it
certainly seems logical as far as we can understand. Jesus
says that our real home, even when on earth, is in heaven.
We are told in the Epistle to the Ephesians to preserve

a sense of balance and proportion while living on earth in the physical body by never forgetting our true citizenship. "Now therefore ye are no more strangers and foreigners, but fellow-citizens with the saints, and of the household of God." (Eph. 2:19). We are eternally constructed and when we have spent some time in a spiritual body we will be able to understand, by contrast, why we had to go through the limitations of the flesh. No one fully understands or appreciates a vacation until he has spent months or years in unrelenting work. Life is built upon a series of backgrounds of light and shade, and a spiritual being, such as you and I are, must learn to appreciate the value of spiritual freedom by knowing the meaning of temporary physical limitation. God made this limitation of the physical world as attractive and beautiful as possible. He filled it with spiritual parables of mystery and wonder so that there is no excuse for anyone to lose sight of his real nature while being limited to a rather clumsy body of earthy construction.

The physical or temporary body is used as an instrument by the real or spiritual body for the purpose of giving outward expression in a passing material world. It is to the spirit what a fountain pen is to the mind. Suppose that you have an idea you want to express via your pen. Should the pen break or become lost, does that mean that you no longer have a mind, feelings, love, and character? Certainly they are not lost just because you lost your fountain pen. If you lose your pen, you get a pencil, or a typewriter, or a dictaphone, or you communicate by word of mouth, or by prayer. The loss of a pen does not silence you forever any more than the loss of a physical body can stop you from living.

In enjoying fellowship with the dead, or, as the Prayer Book puts it, when we "rejoice in their fellowship," we must not think in terms of flesh and bones. You can never see the real "me" as long as you look at me with your physical eyes. You can see my hands, my feet, and my body, you can even see my eyes, through which I look out upon the physical world; but you cannot see the real me which is my soul, my character, my sins, my virtues, and my hopes. Yet, what am I but the sum total of the component parts of my spiritual body which is invisible and indestructible?

Chapter VIII

PARADISE, PURGATORY, HELL,
AND HEAVEN

THE question of where we go, what we do, and how we spend our time after death is potentially controversial. Some churches have dogmatic theories which go far beyond scriptural evidence. Unfortunately, the hellfire and damnation Gospel did much to retard religion in America. People still resent the crass emphasis that stressed a technique of terror. Some churches have worked out a system far beyond the teachings of our Lord or the Bible. They attempt to mechanize one's relationship to the after life. All of these abuses, either on the part of Protestant or Catholic churches, are to be regretted. Yet, there is much evidence concerning the after life. While we cannot be dogmatic about it, we can point to the general teachings of the Bible, of historic Christianity, and of human experience. These beliefs are sane and satisfactory. They should be well known to the whole body of intelligent Christians.

Death is the separation of the soul from the body. Science regards death only as it affects the body; Christians regard it as it touches upon the whole man. Certainly, to lose the physical body is to part with a very wonderful instrument. Most of us have a deep regard for our bodies and, when not carried to an extreme, it is Christian and wholesome. After all, our religion teaches that our bodies are temples for The Spirit. The important thing for the Christian to bear in mind is that there is another body beside the physical. It may seem like a terrible loss to part with the earthly body but St. Paul assures us that this body is not to be compared with the glory of the new spiritual body.

Sentimentalists in religion often teach a vague theory that all people go to heaven when they die. Certainly Our Lord taught that there is judgment and that we must pay for breaking spiritual laws. We are to be judged by our conduct in this life. Account will be taken of the knowledge and opportunities that we have had, and some will unquestionably receive harsher judgment than others. Surely the underprivileged slum child, who has been raised amid crime and filth, will hardly be judged by a merciful God by the same standards as the youngster who has been born into comfort, cleanliness, education, and moral instruction.

The subject of judgment is one that our age does not say much about. We live in an era of crime and widespread sin where "judgment" is hardly a welcome idea. Much of the philosophy of today suggests that you can "get away" with much if you are clever and, therefore, the thought of a day of reckoning is distasteful. This applies both to the rich and to the poor. The Creeds teach that our Lord Himself is to be the one who judges us. From Him "no secrets are hid." He sees right through us at all times. We often fool ourselves into believing that we have outsmarted Him, but we must learn that we cannot break the rules of the universe and evade the cost.

The doctrine of judgment is the only rational approach to the universe and to life. It has been believed by most heathen nations, and was taught by Plato and other great philosophers. The important thing to remember about judgment is that it will be based upon the loving kindness and mercy of our Lord. "He shall come to be our judge." Certainly no one can look at the spirit of His life and believe that He insists upon such distasteful doctrines as eternal damnation for unbaptized babies. It would be equally hard to believe that heaven is the reward for one who makes a death-bed confession after a life of deliberate sin.

It is stated in the Epistle to the Hebrews: "It is appointed unto men once to die, but after this the judgment." And in II Corinthians: "We must all appear before the judgment seat of Christ; that every one may receive the things done in his body, according to that he hath done, whether it be good or bad."

We certainly believe in the resurrection of the body, but that it will not be the same physical body we had on earth. The new body is to be a spiritual body. St. Paul tells us: "It is sown a natural body; it is raised a spiritual body." And, "For this corruptible must put on incorruption, and this mortal must put on immortality." It may have some resemblance to our present body, though in what way we hardly know. We will be able to recognize one another, not so much on a basis of physical form as by traits of personal character.

When it comes to a discussion of hell, we know very little. It may be that there is a place, or a state of complete disintegration, for those who deliberately defy our Lord if they know better within their hearts. Generally, hell is that state or condition whereby we are separated from God and all that is good. Most of us have had moments of such an experience here upon earth. It should not be hard to compare some of our awful hours of remorse, disgrace, and pangs of conscience resultant from unrepented and unforgiven sin, with the possibilities of hell. Just what the unforgivable sin is we do not know, but there probably is such a thing. A real state of hell undoubtedly exists, although it must be far from the old naive pictures of pitchforks, furnaces, and physical tortures. Suffering will be nonetheless real, but of a different nature.

Paradise is generally regarded as a state of growth into which the great mass of Christians enters upon death. In Paradise, the ancient Fathers taught, the departed are making progress toward perfection. There they receive help from friends in the form of prayers, and from their instructors who are probably angels. This state of preparation is a temporary abode of the departed. Heaven is the eventual goal. That our Lord will be tender and understanding to any who wholeheartedly seek Him, regardless of how sad their pasts have been, is evident from His thoughtfulness toward the dying thief upon the cross.

The Latin or Roman Catholic theory is quite different from our traditional belief. Purgatory is a state of purification and is very painful. It differs from hell only in that it is temporary and not eternal. Time to be spent in purgatory, so the Latin theory believes, may be shortened by prayers and masses. In the Roman Church an enormous enterprise has been built up around the practice of saying masses for the dead and from indulgences granted by the Pope which may be applied for their benefit and earlier release from suffering. There seems to be little or no scriptural evidence for such a belief.

Just what heaven will be like is beyond our imagination and knowledge. Certainly it means that we will be with God and that He will have planned a wonderful state of existence for us. But heaven should not be regarded as a far-removed state which we can not know until after the general resurrection. Instead, we should begin to look at eternal life as an experience that can start here and now. Snatches of a sense of being in God's presence can be known in this life for heaven is where God is. Certain glimpses of heaven can be experienced during our times of greatest joys; these times may come through work, family, friends, or service based on personal sacrifice. God wants everyone to attain heaven and He will do anything within His power to get us there. I can never believe that He will not give us every chance of reeducation and training so that we may overcome old and sometimes vicious habits of thought and deed. Heaven probably won't be a place of languid relaxation, nor will it be a continuous concert rendered on golden harps. It will be vital, alive, full of action, humor, love, service, understanding, fearlessness, and joy. Where God is, all the attributes that are worth living for in the natural body will be experienced to the full in the spiritual body.

Chapter IX

CONTINUAL GROWTH

GOD has so ordered the life of man that each individual has certain definite courses mapped out for his soul's experience. Sooner or later, in this earthly life or in Paradise, he must master each assignment. Our Lord has told us that we are to proceed in the direction of perfection. These lessons are not primarily a matter of intellectual obstacles but rather a series of standards of character based on wise spiritual understanding. Just as our Lord grew in stature and in favor with God and man, so are we charged with a like responsibility for growth. The education of the soul can be compared to the grade school pursuits of a child. He has certain courses in specified grades and he passes to the next grade when he has satisfied the requirements of his teacher. Sometimes he misses out entirely and must go back and take the grade over. When he graduates from eighth grade and leaves that particular school, there are a few tears perhaps but there is far greater rejoicing because he has graduated. It is a gala occasion rather than a time to lament. His ambition is realized; he is going to High School. For a while he will not be so closely associated with some of the youngsters he knew in the lower grades but they will be coming along pretty soon; they will be entering High School in a year or two and our old graduate will meet them and "show them the ropes." How proud will the young freshman be to have this Junior or Senior for a guide.

The education of the soul is worked out by God on a fixed, though not legalistic, plan. Where you leave off here on this earth, you begin in Paradise. If you are a spiritual third-grader here, when you pass over, so you will be there. Your credits will be known by the very quality of your inner soul which now is an open book. "Then shall I know even as also I am known." You continue your program of growth without interruption. So there is plenty of work and interest ahead, as well as good times, and perhaps problems. Hence, the Prayer Book directs us to pray: "And we also bless thy holy Name for all thy servants departed this life in thy faith and fear; beseeching thee to grant them continual growth in thy love and service, and to give us grace to follow . . ."

When life on this earth is understood as a school for the growth and development of the soul under the disciplined limitation of a physical body, it somewhat lessens our confusion because of cruelties which crop out in almost every generation. The world goes along with a certain amount of seeming progress and then there comes an outbreak of barbarism which exceeds almost anything we have known before. This throws some people into atheism. They are baffled by the shocking knowledge that the world has made so little progress. Disillusionment follows inevitably. That is too bad. The trouble is in the individual's concept of life on this earth. He thinks that this materialistic world existence is an end in itself. Such a belief is doomed to bitter disappointment.

Jesus said, "Be of good cheer, I have overcome the world." By this statement He did not mean that we should neglect to work assiduously for the betterment of mankind on earth, but He did want us to know that our true citizenship as Christians is in heaven, even when living on earth. We are not to break down in bitterness and despair and allow sin to overcome the world. We are to do all in our power to bring God's eternal Kingdom into as much of the experience of life here as possible.

Back to the school analogy again. Every year, a Senior class graduates and a Freshman class appears and the teachers have to go on teaching the same courses over and over again to new pupils. They do not become discouraged because the incoming class does not know as much as the outgoing class. They expect the new ones to be untaught. But they also know that those who have finished the course must go on, so they rejoice with the graduates and labor with the Freshmen. They take them as they come.

Every new generation that is born into this life on this earth must start where the preceding generation did. At the beginning. They come in with the same basic urges, instincts, wants, impulses, fears, and tendencies toward sin. Those forces must be trained, disciplined, and cultured, just as were those of the earlier generations. One thing we know is that our children do not learn much by our experience; they learn mostly by their own. They learn the hard way, and so must all of us. You see your son making mistakes which you know are going to hurt him and you tell him so, but he doesn't really believe you until he tries the experiment himself. Later, he probably comes around and says, "Dad, you were right." The primary purpose of life in this world is not necessarily to achieve ultimate perfection. It is to give a certain elementary training in the progress of the soul and to prepare that soul for the next school, which, on the cross, our Lord called Paradise.

Chapter X

THE COMMUNION OF SAINTS

THE Church that our Lord established is composed of several parts. First, its personality is like that of Jesus Himself, both human and divine. People frequently forget that. The institution which He established is divine and eternal per se, but the human beings on earth who operate it here are indeed very human and frail. Secondly, the Church is Militant, Expectant, and Triumphant. The Militant Church is composed of those who are still here on earth battling against the world, the flesh, and the devil. The Church Expectant is that part which is in Paradise working toward a more complete cleansing of their souls. The Church Triumphant is that which has arrived at what is commonly known as the Beatific Vision. Its members have completed the course and are at one with God.

The whole Church is known as the Communion of Saints. This is a combination of all of the various branches and aspects. Thus, in reality, we are not part of an institution divided into separate compartments and entities but rather a magnificent unit, worshiping together at the Holy Communion with angels, archangels, and the whole company of heaven. Furthermore, it is important to realize that the total Church membership not only is composed of the millions who inhabit the earth today but also includes the countless hosts of Christians who for the past two thousand years have gone beyond the grave. Therefore, it is exceedingly important that those of us who belong to the small portion of the Church Militant be cognizant of the great Church Expectant and Triumphant; that we be in conscious communion and fellowship with these spiritually advanced divisions through prayer and in the Holy Communion. Here we have "the blessed company of all faithful people."

Therefore, let us not make the mistake of thinking that a saint is merely a great Christian of the past who has been canonized by the Church and given a specific place in our Church Militant calendar year. A Saint of the Church is a member who is trying to practice the faith either in this life or in the one beyond. Therefore, in the larger sense we are all saints, we are all in communion one with another through Christ Himself.

It is important that we have the fact clear in our minds that we are part of a continuous spiritual stream. The Church and the diocese, to which we belong here in our own particular state, is part of the great Expectant and Triumphant Church in the realms beyond. Those of us who are close to our Lord are "in Him" and thus are made one with each other in this all-embracing Christian fellowship. There is no real separation between the earthly parish church or mission and the communities in Paradise and heaven. Since we are with Christ, especially at the Holy Communion, we are likewise with them. They are one with Him and so are we. That is the greater Church unity of which so few of us have any conscious realization. Therefore, you can see why Saints' Days, Anniversaries for the departed, and days commemorating angels, are so vital to the life and oneness of the whole Church. Likewise, the individual who is a participant in this great unity is the recipient of energy and friendship which is stimulating and invaluable.

It is also important to remember that the great majority of the members of the whole Church, those who have passed on in particular, are not yet perfected "in Him." They are saints in the making; they are in the process of arriving at that state of true perfection. Undoubtedly, the great bulk of the whole Church belongs in that inter- mediate state known as Paradise, or the Church Ex- pectant. It is in that state that the constant process of education is being carried on whereby the soul learns to overcome selfishness and sin. There souls are given every possible opportunity to develop and build themselves into Christlike men and women. It is in this process of development, both for us here and for them over there, that we are part of a network of prayer linking each to the other through Jesus Christ our Lord. We do not believe in the abuse of the Medieval Church that "saying so many masses" will automatically catapult people out of hell into a higher realm. We do believe that our prayers for those who have passed on, and their prayers for us, through Christ, are of great benefit each to the other.

This matter of "praying to the saints" is one that we ought to have straightened out in our minds. Certainly it is a superstitious practice to pray to a saint in the sense that he is a minor God and that we are seeking his supernatural assistance. No such concept is held in the traditional faith. We should merely talk to a saint in prayer as to a friend and ask him to think of us when he says his prayers. Time and again people ask me if I will not remember some person who is sick, and naturally I am delighted with the privilege. So also, the people who are in the realm of the Church Expectant or Triumphant can be asked if they will not kindly do the same in their prayers. After all, they have great experience and growth and understanding and why not enlist their friendship and assistance. This is a very ancient practice and it seems to me one that is extremely normal and reasonable. Naturally, when a saint is looked upon as a magical device it is a terrible abuse, and it is against such practices that Protestantism rightly rebels. Again, rebellion should be practiced in the sense of reform rather than complete revolution. In the Eastern Church, all good and holy people are thought of as being able to assist us through their prayers and surely that is a wise and sensible approach. Why shouldn't I frequently remember my dearest friends who have passed on and enlist their assistance from time to time? Surely their interest in me would be sufficient to give me the best of their time, attention, and prayer life at certain periods when I am particularly in need. Thus, we can see that in the doctrine of the Communion of Saints there is a vast and rich reservoir of spiritual energy. An opportunity for our participation in it is one of the greatest privileges offered to mankind. Dr. W. Norman Pittenger, in his book, *His Body the Church*,* seems to me to sum up the spirit of the Communion of Saints in a magnificent paragraph when he states, "It is a tremendous and breathtaking thought—that the whole creation, from star-dust to sanctity, from the dirt of the ground to the ideals in man's breast, from the delicate beauty of the hidden flower to the open glory of the heavens, from the first movement of life to the intimate sharing of our human loving, has its place in a divine scheme and in all its wonderful richness and diversity will also have its ultimate place in the redemption."

The idea of mutual prayer, within the fellowship of the saints, has ample evidence from the very earliest days of Christianity. St. Cyprian, the martyr-Bishop of Carthage, who was born in the century after St. John's death (A.D. 200), made an agreement with his friend Cornelius that whichever of them died first should remember the one who remained behind, "Let us mutually be mindful of each other . . . . on both sides let us always pray for each other, let us relieve our affections and distresses by a reciprocity of love, and whichever of us goes hence before

* Morehouse-Gorham Co. By permission.

the other by the speed of the divine favor, let our affections continue before the Lord."

A contemporary of St. Cyprian, named Origen, one of the greatest of all Christian scholars, says, "All the souls who have departed this life, still retaining their love for those who are in the world, concern themselves for their salvation and aid them by their prayers and meditation with God . . . . It is my opinion that all these fathers who have fallen asleep before us, fight on our side and aid us by their prayers." The early fathers of the Church were unanimous in their references to this intercommunion between all of the Saints in the great Universal Church.

Chapter XI

SHALL WE TELL THEM THE TRUTH?

IT IS too bad that good Church people are so rarely instructed sufficiently in the Church's doctrine of Immortality. Few face death with calm confidence and quiet assurance. The blame, as a rule, rests with the clergyman who has not taught the faith. It has been my frequent experience to go into sick rooms, where the patients were expected to die, and to have the families caution me to say nothing that would make the sufferers aware of the seriousness of their condition. The families to which I refer are often Church members in good standing. Time and again so-called Christians neither want their loved ones to face the truth, nor do they themselves believe enough in the central theme of Christianity to have faith in the Resurrection. On the other hand, the tactful but honest approach which comes after prayer for guidance by the Holy Spirit is almost the greatest comfort a dying person can have.

Right now, as I write this book, a charming elderly lady is dying a slow death from a dread disease in a nearby hospital. The family did not think it wise to discuss death with her but when they invited me to call on her, they did not limit my visit by saying, "Don't let her know how badly off she is." When I did see her, it took only a few minutes for her to talk about her death as imminent. How foolish it would have been for me to try to talk her out of it. She faced the prospect with me quite calmly and without emotion. I told her that she could undoubtedly be of great service to her family in her next life because of the new clarity of her vision and the greater understanding she would have in saying her prayers. I also talked to her about her continual growth in the next life, and her new opportunities there. She not only paid great attention to what I had to say but she was delighted and relieved.

When I was rector of Gethsemane Church, Minneapolis, a parishioner was dying from a long and lingering disease and it was my privilege to call on her many times. She wanted to talk about death, which we did, and, as usual, the patient received great mental relief as well as spiritual comfort, even to the point of light-heartedness. When the end was near I called on her again and she asked me to pray that she be permitted to live for three more days. When I asked why, she stated that several of her family were coming home and she wanted to live until they arrived because she had helpful things to tell them. I saw no reason why such a request could not be made, and offered the petition. When all the family had arrived and had conversed with her, she slipped off into a coma from which such cases rarely arouse. I received a phone call informing me of her condition and went out to the house. I stood at the foot of her bed for a minute and prayed for her quiet bodily release, but to my amazement her breathing became strong and she opened her eyes and looked at me with a wonderful smile and said, "I knew you'd come before I went. Thanks so much for the prayer. I talked to them all, and I feel quite relieved. Give me the Blessing and then I'll go." I walked to the side of her bed, took her hand and asked her please to remember me when she arrived on the other side as I certainly would need her clear vision and prayers. She nodded assurance, and smiled. I gave her the Final Blessing and she slipped away.

How much better it is, wherever possible, to give the dying a preparation which will let them go on in the truth rather than in a state of fear. Think of it from the angle of the dying person. Have they not a right to the truth? Too often, the family that tries to protect the patient from a desired discussion of death is not trying to protect the dying, but themselves. They are sincere but misguided.

Death is the one factor which every human soul must inevitably face and the sooner we bring it out into the open the better off we will all be. When we link up the two worlds of the seen and the unseen by the Sacrament of the Holy Communion and by prayers which set up an intercommunication system, we will be well on the way toward Christian maturity and psychological security.

Of course, the best way to handle this whole matter is to have family discussions of the subject when everyone is quite well and normal. The matter should not be put off until desperate illness occurs. But we warn against the extreme foolishness of those who come into sick rooms with a "Prepare to Meet Thy God" attitude. It is bad to force a sick person to face the subject of death when he has no desire to do so. The discussion must always start from the patient, never from the visitor. Talk over death when you are all well, and use great wisdom with one who is sick, but when the patient so desires, face it.

Chapter XII

WHAT ABOUT THE MENTALLY SICK?

WHEN the insane pass away do they remain insane? I do not believe so. I am firmly convinced that there is a definite difference between the soul and the physical brain. Secular psychologists have no pronouncements to make on this subject, and rightly so, for it is out of their field; but he who has ministered to the mentally ill in things of the spirit has a right to speculate, on the basis of personal experience. During the early part of my ministry I was chaplain at the State Hospital for the Insane, as well as of the Psychiatric Ward of Cook County Hospital in Chicago. What impressed me was the power religious services have over people who otherwise often are uncontrollable.

I regularly held services for about two thousand inmates, who suffered from almost every type of insanity. On a few occasions, I have seen strange displays of abnormal actions but, for the most part, the services, for which I prayed and prepared, were as orderly as those in the parishes I visit now. (After all, insanity is supposed to be only a matter of degree.) Yet, this was a State Institution which refused to take patients unless they were definitely deranged and too difficult for their families to manage. An intelligent conversation seldom could be carried on with the patients because of their distorted brains, but certainly we had definite results with their spiritual natures.

On a number of occasions I have held private services of the Holy Communion for a handful of patients in the wards, and always I have had a distinct feeling that God was accomplishing His purpose, for during the service one could tell that the soul was registering, even though the brain might not remember after the service. People so often asked why I did this work and wondered if it was not a waste of time. My answer is that no more fruitful ministry have I ever experienced.

I feel that when the mentally ill leave their tired and worn bodies, the temporary blanket of insanity will fall away and reveal the real state of the soul. In many instances, the soul will be far along in its education. It is so common for us to think only in terms of ministering to temporary bodies and brains rather than to eternal souls and minds. Thus, we must never give up spiritual ministrations to the insane, even though their physical brains do not seem to register. I repeat, that amongst the hundreds of those to whom I have given the Sacrament, and for whom I have offered prayer, I have almost never been without a real sense of their spiritual benefit. Often it was more than a feeling or sensing on my part, it was a matter of knowing.

So many people who are skeptical about immortality

anxiously ask, "But how can a soul function without a physical brain?" The answer is that the spiritual body which is promised us in the Bible will undoubtedly be more adequate than the most perfect physical body. But some man will say, "How are the dead raised up? and with what body do they come? Thou fool, that which thou sowest is not quickened except it die . . . . It is sown in corruption; it is raised in incorruption: It is sown in dishonour; it is raised in glory: It is sown in weakness; it is raised in power: It is sown a natural body; it is raised a spiritual body. There is a natural body, and there is a spiritual body . . . . Now this I say, brethren, that flesh and blood cannot inherit the kingdom of God; neither doth corruption inherit incorruption. Behold, I shew you a mystery; We shall not all sleep, but we shall all be changed, In a moment, in the twinkling of an eye, at the last trump: for the trumpet shall sound, and the dead shall be raised incorruptible, and we shall be changed. For this corruptible must put on incorruption, and this mortal must put on immortality . . . . Therefore, my beloved brethren, be ye stedfast, unmoveable, always abounding in the work of the Lord, forasmuch as ye know that your labour is not in vain in the Lord."

Chapter XIII

SPECULATIONS ON SUFFERING

IF, IN the new after-physical world, we are not to have material bodies, what kind of suffering might we experience? Before discussing the question, let us first state that God does not deliberately inflict pain. Pain generally comes as the result of wilfully, or unknowingly, breaking God's laws. Thus, the sinner often causes the innocent to suffer and for the most part we can not understand this. God must have some good reason. Sin causes God to be sorrowful. Our pain causes Him to suffer with us even as He has already suffered humiliation and crucifixion for us. It hurts Him to see us hurt ourselves and others. He has given us His laws, standards, and precepts, the laws of His universe and of human relationships. He has provided us with the means of grace and supernatural aid, so that we will have the strength to keep His commands. He has done everything in His power to prevent our pain and suffering. Here are a few ways in which we could find life in a spiritual world rather difficult if we were wedded to the standards of a physical world.

Dependence upon physical appetites for the essence of our earthly enjoyment will place us in a sad vacuum when we take on our spiritual bodies. These new bodies are promised in the Bible and so have always been taken for granted. "For I know that if this earthly tent that I live in now is taken down, God will provide me a building in heaven to live in, not built by human hands but eternal . . . I shall never find myself disembodied." (Goodspeed, II Cor. 5:3.) So, on the one hand, while the new spiritual body will have many new perceptions and means of joy, on the other it will be devoid of some that we too greatly depend upon in earthly life. It will be hard for the person who lived for lust, sex, food, physical thrill, and sensate pleasures to adjust to the new body. By this I do not mean to intimate that sensory pleasures are all intrinsically wrong, for many enjoy them in their proper and legitimate places, but when we love them to the exclusion of all else we are then slaves to that which will surely pass from us. When we are denied them, where are we? One might say in hell. To any heavy smoker who has tried to give up cigarettes for Lent, we need say no more.

Another thought of the possible pain we might experience in the next world would stem from a fascination for the sins of the spirit which would tend to isolate us from great souls. We might be near them, yet separated by a great gulf. If one's soul had been fed for the most part on resentment, jealousy, hatred, meanness, and self-righteousness, one would feel quite painfully out of place in the presence of spiritual adults. Have you ever been alone in a foreign country, unable to speak or even understand the language? That can be a form of hell.

We may expect that our method of communication will be by thought. You will be an open book. You will be recognized, not by what you look like, but by what you really are. How would you like it here on earth if when you walked into the office all that went on in your thoughts was an open book to the boss, to the office boy, to the stenographer, to the salesgirl? Even worse, what if every thought was open to every member of your family, especially to your children? These speculations have possibilities and it is well to ponder the pain of the spirit which some day we may gather unto ourselves. Certainly, no pain to the body could quite touch the possible sufferings that may come to the heart and mind. Fear may not be the highest motive for righteousness but it is a way of making us sensible enough to escape a most unpleasant future by the practical means which our Lord provided through His Church. She stands ever ready to prepare the soul for the future through repentance and absolution.

The classic study on the subject of suffering is to be found in the Book of Job. It discusses the general question "why should the righteous suffer?" The problem of evil has rarely been dealt with adequately and, perhaps, on this earth never will be fully answered. The Book of Job tells us that personal troubles are not necessarily due to one's own wrong-doing. We are to think of life in terms of service to Almighty God without any idea of personal reward—serve Him for His own sake. The greater we conceive God to be, the less becomes the problem of personal pain. Job is a symbol of Israel in her period of captivity. The book has two introductory chapters and four chapters of debate on this timeless question.

In the beginning, we find Job living happily with his family. Then comes a series of troubles which cannot be explained. He endures them all with fortitude, and is visited by three friends who would console him. They cannot but feel that his suffering is due to his own wickedness. Job stedfastly protests his innocence. At last, his confidence begins to crack and he cries out against God. Then a bystander, Elihu, steps in, declaring that all of them are wrong in their analysis of the situation. He declares that the justice of God can never be judged by an analysis of one man's pain. He shows them that earthly judgment is totally inadequate to an understanding of the discipline that man must experience. Finally, out of the whirlwind God Himself speaks. He points out His providential guidance for all of His creation. Job, with great humility, answers the Lord, saying, "I know that thou canst do everything, ... and that no thought can be withholden from thee. . . . . . . Therefore have I uttered that I understood not . . . . . things too wonderful for me, which I knew not . . . . . . but now mine eye seeth thee . . . . . Wherefore I abhor myself, and repent in dust and ashes." Thus the great study concludes and Job is restored to happiness, having learned the magnificent lesson of humility.

Chapter XIV

DIVINE DEMOCRACY

THE Gospels offer repeated evidence as testimony to the democracy of God's Kingdom. The judgments of the world are false, our Lord tells us. Men on earth will always tend to judge one another on a basis of bank-balances, holdings, houses, clothes, cars, political or economic power, planes, and yachts. Or, if not sticking to the standard based on material possessions, they will judge on a basis of secular education, race, religion, social background, ancestry, culture clichés, pulchritudinal assets, and charm. In fact, most of us spend the greater part of our time wanting to acquire these things and it is only natural that they should become our general standard of human evaluation. Our Lord assures us, however, that the standards of God are based upon a different set of requirements. In this matter we are told that: "We brought nothing into this world, and it is certain we can carry nothing out" save those qualities of character such as love, truth, wisdom, goodness, simplicity, humility, courage, and generosity.

Some forty-five years ago, in the Diocese of Pittsburgh, there was founded a monastic order of lay brothers known as the St. Barnabas' Brotherhood, whose life vows of poverty, chastity, and obedience are consecrated especially to the service of incurable and penniless men and boys. The philosophy of the Home sweeps aside the standards of the world, for the less a man possesses, in addition to his incurable disease, the better his chance of being admitted. It is a little corner of the Kingdom of Heaven on earth.

One day, the Brother Founder, a dynamic mixture of sainthood, humor, passion, and business acumen, was preaching to one of the congregations in the city. Brother Hance reached the climax with these words: "You're lovely people, but you are too comfortable. You have too many clothes, too many cars, too many houses. But watch out, someday they are going to wheel—yes, wheel—you down this long aisle and then you will stand before the Lord, just the way you are, with nothing but your naked soul. And when that day comes, only the Lord can help you."

A symbolic tradition relative to the equal state of the souls of men before God was established at St. Paul's Cathedral in Buffalo. No floral pieces are allowed in the church at funeral services, regardless of how important the deceased may have been. Two vases of appropriate flowers are placed on the high altar, and possibly a spray upon the casket, but otherwise the vast truckloads of flowers which appear at some funerals are not allowed inside the Cathedral. Sometimes a family is upset because they do not quite see why the rule should be so strictly adhered to, but the majority of communicants, including those who would be likely to have enormous orders of flowers sent to their beloved dead, would have it no other way. While I was Dean, I conducted three funerals within a few days which presented a great contrast, in social and economic standards, but not before the altar of God. The first service was for a great and good citizen who was very rich, the second was for a lovely lady whose husband was a leading figure in the American political scene, and the third was for an old retired negro janitor. In each instance our service and floral decorations were identical, for God is no respecter of persons and before His eyes we all stand as sinners who need forgiveness.

To return to Brother Hance and the humble citizens of St. Barnabas' Home: There is a story that I like to tell which always makes me feel the power of faith in the good works of the departed who "die in the Lord," regardless of superficial possessions. When I first went to visit the St. Barnabas' Home at Gibsonia, I was given dinner and afterward made a pilgrimage with the Brothers to the Blessed Sacrament Chapel. After prayers and the Divine Praises, I lingered to look around. The walls were almost completely covered with names. Brother Hance told me that on those walls are over a thousand names. They represent the men who have passed away in the Home. He went on to say, "Yes, we prepared every one for his death. They are the greatest power we have today—poor men, sick men, crippled men, tired men, but now they are free men—all praying for our work. Think what that means to us."

When we leave this physical world of superficial judgments we are going to be in for a shock. Prejudices based on color, race, possessions, attraction, customs, rituals, ancestors, and living-quarters are going to mean little or nothing. In the Divine Democracy, the superficials will be swept aside and standards of character, service, love, truth, understanding, and humility will be uppermost. How tragic to awaken in Paradise, only to discover that you have spent a lifetime traveling toward a false goal on the wrong highway.

Chapter XV

FACULTIES OF THE SPIRITUAL BODY

WE MIGHT look at the spiritual body as an entity which, of itself, has certain faculties that are operable in or out of the physical body. Those wonderful new senses which the spiritual body will develop in Paradise are not all necessarily unused while we live in the flesh. The history of mystical experience is packed full of factual evidence substantiating the use of spiritual faculties which are far beyond the rational processes of the human brain and the five senses. The Old Testament Prophets, the early Christians, and the Saints of the Church have witnessed innumerable times to the hearing of the Divine Voice, the sight of mystical manifestations and signs, the overcoming of the limits of time and space, gifts of prophecy and healing, as well as many other abilities which defy description and are entirely outside the realm of the physical faculties. Through these higher senses, which are nurtured and developed in meditation and prayer, we can actually practice the Communion of Saints by the help of the Eucharistic Presence and the prayers of the Church. While few will ever have startling mystical experience, all can have the divine comfort of a sense of unity with the departed loved ones by the means provided in the

Church. We will deal further with this subject later on. At the moment, it is enough to call attention to those spiritual gifts or senses, seldom used, which we might just as well start to develop here and now for our own spiritual growth and inter-world communication.

It is necessary for the individual who would grow in spiritual understanding first to regard himself as a spiritual being who temporarily dwells in a house called a physical body. "Though this body be destroyed, yet shall I see God." Some day you will move out of this house into another type of home, brand new and almost impossible to imagine as long as you live only in the material world. Most of us, unfortunately, think of ourselves as bodies and brains and not much else. When in prayer you or I reach the point at which we can objectify ourselves apart from our bodies and look upon them as homes or serviceable instruments over which the real eternal "I," with God's grace, has control, we will have little trouble in sensing the unity which can be had, through our Lord, with other souls now living apart from the flesh. Jesus, of course, had a profound sense of mastery and supervision over His earthly temple, for He said that in three days He would raise another.

The Church has always believed that through Christ there could be a form of communion with the physically departed. The experience of millions of souls through the Christian ages testifies to this fact, but we live in an age when many so-called religious people still find it almost

beyond reason to believe. Scientific data, such as come
from Dr. Joseph B. Rhine and his staff at Duke University,
ought to make us realize that there is a realm which tran-
scends the senses we already know about. Dr. Alexis
Carrel, the Nobel Prize winner and a member of the most
distinguished medical societies in the world, says in his
book, *Man the Unknown*,* "telepathy is a primary datum
of scientific observation . . . . . a normal although rare
activity of human beings . . . . . Many possess it in a
rudimentary state. They use it without effort and in a
spontaneous fashion. Telepathic communications occur
frequently." Thus it should not be too difficult a step from
this earthly stage to a normal and higher communion between free spiritual beings. However, the wholesome and
authorized way is that in which our Lord is the means of
unity and His Sacrament of the Altar the place of meeting.

Katherine Cornell is a communicant of my former
parish and through her I had the privilege of meeting and
becoming a friend of her close companion, Helen Keller.
If one ever wonders about the existence of a spiritual body
which can overcome the limitations of the physical body,
such questions would soon disappear after knowing this
great woman who, when only nineteen months old, was
deprived, through illness, of speech, sight, and hearing.
The persistence with which she has developed her soul
sensitivities lifts one who observes her into a new realm of
experience. She sees, hears, converses, and understands in

* Harper & Brothers. By permission.

a world that is far more real to her than the one by which most of us are overcome. At first I could do nothing but sit and gaze at her amazing beauty, which it not so much the result of physical endowment as, rather, the result of years of study and meditation on things of the spirit. She is at all times alive to a life of unseen reality all about her. Her record is more eloquent and convincing than anything that I could possibly say or write.

In her book, *Let Us Have Faith*,* Miss Keller states: "Faith, like philosophy, endows me with a unity I miss in the chaos of material experience devoid of sight or hearing. But like everyone else I have eyes in my soul. Through faith I create the world I gaze upon; I make my own day and night, tint the clouds with iridescent fires, and behold! a midnight is strewn with other stars. . . . Faith penetrates this dungeon with an optimism that sees the Creator's image in every human being and a determination to expand his capabilities to the utmost through suitable teaching and helpful environment.

"Reason hardly warranted Annie Sullivan's attempt to transform a little half-human, half-animal, deaf, blind child into a complete thing. Neither science nor philosophy has set such a goal, but faith, the eye of love, did. I did not know I had a soul. Then the God in a wise heart drew me out of nothingness with cords of human love and the life belt of language, and lo! I found myself.

"Faith—Annie Sullivan's and mine, and that of all who

* Doubleday & Co., Inc. By permission.

wrought with us—has made my limitations ineffectual if not trivial. And since I have the privilege of doing it, I am proud to bear this testimony to the power of faith . . . . faith is the red blood that braces when all else fails.

"Through faith alone can I fulfil the two senses I lack —sight and hearing—and build out from my imperfect speech. Faith has the ingenuity to bring me insight, and I know where I am going."

"Faith does not oblige us to be unusually endowed, but receptive. To say others may have it but we cannot is wanton self-limitation. To be alert for whatever surprises may glow within us is to have at our command a zest for living, which outweighs all material possessions. Stepping inwardly softly so as not to crush shy dreams and impulses, we shall marvel as our minds little by little disclose the completeness and oneness we potentially are."

"I have unshakeable belief that mankind's higher nature is on the whole still dormant. The greater souls reveal excellencies of mind and heart which their lesser fellows possess—hidden, it is true, but there all the same."

We may not know much as yet about the potential faculties of the soul. But there is sufficient evidence through the saints of the past and great souls of the present, like Helen Keller, to assure us that exciting, thrilling new adventure awaits us when we start life completely independent of the earthly physical body in which we have spent our lives so far on this earth. Yet, that adventure is not necessarily postponed until the death of the body but can begin any time that we desire to launch out into the mystery of prayer and meditation through the Church's many avenues of spiritual technique.

Because of the evidence of the spiritual abilities of many highly developed mystical Christians throughout the ages, it is more than likely that we may have now the rudiments of faculties by which we shall later live when we have left our bodies. Man has discovered wireless telegraphy, television, and radio communications for a material machine. It is probable that something akin to them already exists within each soul for men and women have so frequently demonstrated these abilities in states of spiritual ecstasy, meditation, and prayer. We are just scratching the surface of some of these qualities in current laboratory studies. They have produced convincing evidences of extrasensory perception and kindred scientific discoveries. Already, three men have received the Nobel Prize for research in electrical brain waves. While the detailed nature of these new-found psychic powers are not yet fully known, they do point to the fact that the brain is at all times a broadcasting station and that emotions and moods can actually be recorded. One of the leaders in this field of research, Dr. Edgar Douglas Adrian, a British Nobel Prize winner, says that the technique of brain wave measurement has been so advanced that it can now be charted with accuracy to a thousandth of a second. This is done by placing electrodes against the head and thus picking up the electrical currents of the mind, amplifying them and recording them on a graph. The mysteries of the emotions are thereby recorded and studied and so carry the scientist very close to the intangibles of human character and to the things of the spirit.

Just what kind of faculties we will have is still a mystery, as far as after-death experience is concerned, but we already know that prayer, meditation, and sacramental devotions will take us into a dimension that is out beyond the senses, which reaches into a new world "not built with hands, eternal in the heavens."

Before leaving this section of our subject, let us have a perfectly clear understanding that these spiritual faculties by which we shall eventually live outside our earthly bodies are not to be thought of as abnormal any more than are some of the modern inventions like radio and radar. The laws for these seeming modern miracles have existed since God created the universe. The laws of radio activity were always there. We merely did not fully understand them. For centuries, man has known many of the great principles of prayer which are so akin to our modern forms of mechanical thought transmission. Jesus promised that we should do even greater things than are evidenced in the New Testament. We will develop understanding of the myriad laws and mysteries that He waits to unfold when we have sought and knocked with sufficient intensity to warrant their manifestation. These spiritual faculties which are even now available, in part, are healthy and normal segments of the total personality. We need never be afraid of them or of their use unless our motives be selfish. As long as we seek to use them in complete surrender to His will, we are in His hands. For the Christian with vision, faith, and hope, great days are always ahead.

Chapter XVI

GOOD AND EVIL ANGELS

THE Christian concept of eternity would hardly be complete without the teaching about angels. Frequent reference is made to the ministry of angels throughout the Bible and particularly in the New Testament. Our Lord not only believed in them but taught us of their practical helpfulness. To ignore their place in the Christian scheme of things would be to leave out one of the teachings of the historic Church and her Bible. We shall proceed in this chapter to summarize what the Bible and the Church generally believe, although there is a widespread difference of emphasis on this theme and no one can be dogmatic.

Who and what are angels? For the most part, they mean little to the present-day Christian. We seem to regard them as mythical people who wander through a terrestrial world with cumbersome wings, flowing robes, and sentimentally sweet-sounding harps. Mid-Victorian artists have filled our churches with stained-glass windows which depict a race of beings whom the world has regarded as part of our folklore and fairytale inheritance. These pictures of human beings with harps and wings have somehow helped to discourage our belief in the true character of these wonderful creatures of God. The Bible describes them as appearing in the form of men, without wings; they appear with wings only in the Apocalyptic passages.

According to the Bible and the traditional interpretation of the Church, angels are people somewhat like ourselves. They are highly intelligent and are regarded as being more astute and keen than we, with certain gifts beyond those which we possess. God made us a little "lower than the angels." They also are reported to have free will. They can choose between right and wrong, and because of this fact they are divided into two great groups, the good and the evil angels. Wherever free will exists there is always the opportunity to defy God and to break spiritual law. This is what happened in their world. One of their hierarchy, through the sin of pride and jealousy, led a revolt. Milton, in *Paradise Lost*, attributes this revolt to the ambition of the leader who was jealous of the position of our Lord. Whether or not Milton's speculation is correct, it is obvious that the sin of lust for power possessed the minds of a sufficient number to start an insurrection. Thereby the vast host of beings whom God had created for the purpose of helping in the realm of the unseen was split.

Traditional theology has sometimes divided good angels into three great groups. The first are known as "Thrones," composed of Cherubim and Seraphim. It is held that their work is to serve the Holy Trinity and to carry out the special duties attendant to the divine realm. The second group is known as "Dominions," being composed of Virtues and

Powers. These angels, it is said, are assigned to the process and developments of nature and to a ministry of helpfulness among the unfortunate in the wars of the world. The third group is called "Principalities," composed of Angels and Archangels. Their reported duties are especially with human beings who dwell upon earth, to serve them and to assist them in their prayers and to aid them when they pass from the physical body to Paradise.

Before we think about the positive association and value of the realms of good angels, it is important that we give some consideration to those who serve with the forces of evil. It should not be difficult to convince anyone of the powerful reality of the statement in I Peter 5:8 which says, "be vigilant; because your adversary the devil, as a roaring lion, walketh about, seeking whom he may devour." The devil and his clever assistants, so well described in *The Screwtape Letters* of C. S. Lewis, may not wear the traditional red suits nor carry pitchforks, but they certainly have instruments of evil far more effective than those that we have heard about in sentimental Sunday School papers. The devil does not deal in gadgets which burn the flesh, and instruments that torture the body; he deals in thoughts that poison the mind, in ideas that bring cancer to the soul, in hatreds that cause war and death to plague the innocent. He receives far more satisfaction out of a living slave who thinks he is free than out of an enslaved body which would rather be dead.

The radio sends out ideas in the form of waves, which

can be picked up and amplified by a receiving set, and it is certain that the devil can too, as the Bible and Church have always taught. It is his business to send forth corrupt ideas to contaminate unsurrendered minds. The Bible tells us that the very air about us carries evil emanations, as well as good, which are looking for easy mental lodgings at all times. The forces of evil never let up with their subtle propaganda, which they spread, not only in the places of iniquity where they have already won the battle, but also—and particularly—in the places of respectability, and even in the Sanctuary of God. They are constantly carrying the battle to the Christian stronghold, especially in these days of destructive theological standards. There are some highly educated critics of the Bible and the Church who started out with honest desires to correct the errors of a too literal Bible fundamentalism. Who knows but that the devil cleverly maneuvered them into bolstering up the religious debunkers? The time when we must be especially cautious concerning the forces of evil is when we think that we are most righteous, holy, and intellectually self-sufficient. No situation so conditions the devil's activity as spiritual and mental pride.

So the Church has taught that devils are angels who rebelled against the will of God. When our Lord went out to make His great decision in the wilderness, there also went Satan with his assistants. During those forty days, there took place the greatest spiritual struggle of all history. At that time, Jesus taught us the principles by which we can win the same war now, for it goes on continually the world over. The same bait is held out today that was offered then—the bait of pride, power, and avarice. Our Lord warned us of the brilliant tactics of the evil one, who watches for the time when we become penitent and cast out our besetting sins through the power of the Holy Ghost, and then, inwardly swept and garnished, over-confidently ignore the still existing dangers the devil subtly puts before us. Jesus said it is then we must beware. If we have not replaced with some positive substitute the negative power which was eliminated, far worse evils will usurp the vacancy. This is a danger not to be compared with most of the things we spend our time worrying about. When we rid self or the world of an evil dictator, we must be careful lest a far worse man come to take his place. He may arrive outwardly championing the cause of democracy but underneath he may be working for the enslavement of us all.

Until I was a chaplain in the Insane Asylum, which I have previously mentioned, I had never thought much about demoniac possession. But after I had spent a number of months visiting in the various wards of that institution I was forced to consider the ancient teachings. Some causes for insanity can be treated successfully by medical science, but a large group of mentally disturbed and nervously distraught patients who hear voices, have queer illusions and hallucinations, are beyond the help of science. Yet I have seen the powerful effect of positive prayer, when our Lord was called upon, free individuals from the forces that possessed them.

The forces of evil are far from being a loosely knit band of marauders; indeed, they are organized, well trained, and disciplined. A vicious war is constantly being waged between these good and these evil entities; a battle for the possession of the mind of man here on earth. We can have protection, however. There is no need for fear if we stay close to God. His power is at all times sufficient to keep us in safety. If we do not believe in the need of protection, what is our answer to the forces that used Hitler and Hirohito to bring suffering and despair to over half the world in this past war? We still naively believe that we can save the world by conferences and pacts alone. War starts with evil thoughts, and evil thoughts can't be stopped by guns and pacts, but, rather, through prayer after the will, as far as possible, is offered to God.

Listen to this splendid description in Ephesians 6: 10-12. "Be strong in the Lord, and in the power of his might. Put on the whole armour of God, that ye may be able to stand against the wiles of the devil. For we wrestle not against flesh and blood, but against principalities, against powers, against the rulers of the darkness of this world, against spiritual wickedness in high places. Wherefore take unto you the whole armour of God, that ye may be able to withstand in the evil day, and having done all, to stand."

One of the most effective prayers for the world of our day is the ancient collect, from the Book of Common Prayer, for St. Michael and All Angels' Day. "O Everlasting God, who hast ordained and constituted the services of Angels and men in a wonderful order; Mercifully grant that, as thy holy Angels always do thee service in heaven, so, by thy appointment, they may succour and defend us on earth; through Jesus Christ our Lord. Amen." We always have St. Michael and his angel host to do battle for us.

Angels are spiritual personalities with power in the realm of the unseen. If we can learn to conceive of personality as a combination of those qualities which God wishes us to have, namely, such qualities as wisdom, love, truth, vision, understanding, and Divine Energy, we will be able to cease thinking of angels in materialistic terms. Angels are not limited by time or space, but operate through the medium of thought, attitudes, and desires. Our Lord said that a spirit-born man becomes like the wind. He is free to go and come without physical means of transport.

Angels are referred to as personalities who are warriors of formidable fighting capacity. So we can well eliminate the languid feminine emphasis of the stained-glass windows, and ask for their strengthening and intelligent aid in the daily battle that goes on all around us.

To establish a habit of beginning and ending each day with a thought of thanks to one's personal guardian angel is to establish a custom that soon gives one a great sense of companionship. None of us quite knows who they are, how they operate and what they are like, but the Bible and the Church say they exist to assist us and it seems to me that we had better use all the spiritual aid we can get.

Chapter XVII

ANGELS WANT TO WORK FOR YOU

GOD has provided each of us with guides or angels who are constantly willing to assist us. This was witnessed by Jesus Himself in His temptation in the wilderness, when "Angels came and ministered unto him." Also, if you remember, at the time of His temptation in the garden of Gethsemane, "There appeared an angel unto him from heaven, strengthening him."

It is highly reasonable, as well as practical, that we call upon our Guardian Angels for help. From the point of view of the angels, it must be difficult to be assigned to an individual whom you are supposed to help by suggestions, signs, warnings, and constructive criticisms, only to be ignored during an entire earthly life-span. To realize that we have Guardian Angels is greatly to enhance their ability to be of personal aid. The more you acknowledge them, the more they are able to help you. Remember that they can see more clearly than you can.

As you condition your subconscious to their constant presence, you ready yourself for their subtleties of expression. You become sensitized to their constant attempts to assist you. Angels, like radar and television, will work for us if we will but sensitize our God-given equipment through prayer. A practice which unites many with them is that of pausing briefly in the Communion Service after the phrase "With Angels and Archangels." Acknowledgment at that moment brings a consciousness of the wonderful unity between the two worlds.

The aid of angels has come to mean a great deal to me for I know that in many a tight place they have come to my rescue. They will give you a fighting chance by amazing assistance if they know that you are seeking to repent and are trying to offer your life in the service of Christ. I have often felt like a pitcher on the mound, with bases loaded and two out and a slugger at bat, who pokes one far out into left field. The fielder runs after the ball and makes a circus catch which saves me, yet I get credit for the game. Spiritual assists by Guardian Angels are common occurrences. You may stumble along, and yet if they are convinced that you are moving in the direction of surrender to Christ, trying hard to win the game, they seem to carry you with untold patience. Certainly St. Augustine must have had the help of angels, in addition to the prayers of his mother, during his long period of contemplated conversion.

The actual appearance of angels in mystical manifestations is not an infrequent experience even in our day and generation. Instances of such experiences came out of the second World War and are far beyond the ability of either psychologists or theologians to explain. Sergeant John Bartek, with whom I wrote a book, was on a raft with Captain Rickenbacker, and had such experiences not once but several times. They were in connection with his sister who had died the day before they left on that ill-fated flight. The appearance came to him with such conviction and force that from then on he was carried through the whole night-marish raft experience with a strength that he had never known before. This, in spite of the fact that he had salt-water ulcers, was without food and water, and was in the midst of pain, tragedy, and death. When he reached that part of the story, as he told it to me soon after his release from the hospital, there was a look of powerful conviction about him which made doubt, on my part, impossible.

Soon after I became Bishop of Pittsburgh, I was asked to make a call on a woman who was pathetically crippled by arthritis. It was the day before Christmas and I was pushed for time. It was difficult to locate the house. Finally, I came upon it in an area of tragic housing, walked up the steep steps, and rang the bell in a hurried, impatient mood. A woman appeared and took me up two more flights to a single back room. There lay the woman who had been bed-ridden for eight years. She had often heard me on the radio and was anxious to tell me her story. Her elderly husband was only partially employed but he was away from her much of the time. They shared this one room, and for years she dreaded being left alone. She was so helpless that in case of an emergency or fire she would have been beyond any kind of self-aid. Day after day in her long, lonely hours, she lay there in a semi-paralysis of mental fear and physical contortion. More and more, however, she felt God present as she prayed, and one day, about five years before my visit, she had an experience that changed her whole life. In the midst of her prayers, which had followed a period of unusually deep depression, she heard the squeaky door slowly open. Instinctively, her eyes moved in its direction and a figure of great luminous beauty came in. It came over to her bedside and stood with a tender but confident smile, giving the crippled woman an energy that she had never before felt. She was finally able to speak, and asked the meaning of the visit. The voice answered, "You need never fear, I will always be with you." Whereupon the visitor slowly disappeared. For the five subsequent years and through many lonely hours she no longer worried about being alone. When she told me the story her confidence was not to be questioned. She insisted that there was no element of the dream in her experience but rather that it was an actual visit by her Guardian Angel.

These are but two of the many such experiences about which I have heard. We would hear many more if we had the confidence of those who have known them. They are afraid we might laugh and, sadly enough, some of us would. Experiences of this kind have occurred all through the history of mankind and the evidence is too overwhelming to dismiss as mere hallucination. The point of the two occurrences which I know of personally is that, in each instance, the people who saw the angels were changed from that day forward and have henceforth exhibited a belief that cannot be shaken.

Angels can be regarded as "agents." The late Dr. Francis J. Hall, the great theologian of the General Theological Seminary in New York, so referred to them and the term is probably as good as any. An "Angel" in warfare is one who visits, investigates, and inspects the territory of the enemy and then returns home with the necessary information and strategy for future warfare. All of us can receive much information from Guardian Angels. We are at all times in the midst of great battles, which are being fought against the forces of evil, and our guardians are more than willing to investigate the motives and objectives of the enemy and report back to us in the form of promptings, intuitions, and subtle warnings. Yet, I would not want the reader to feel that every time we call upon our Guardian Angels we will have direct spiritual contact in the concrete form of a message. The great majority will not have any such experience, nor should they expect to. Nevertheless, I believe that delicate promptings are given us more often than we realize. It is merely a matter of being spiritually able to discern "the signs of the times." To attain this degree of awareness we must "pray without ceasing," which means to be always on the spiritual alert.

It is interesting that the spirit of the collect for St. Michael and All Angel's Day is one of assured assistance if we will but believe in their ministry. The Gospel tells us fittingly that all spiritual growth must be built on an attitude which is expressed in the phrase "Except ye become as a little child." A child listens to a story with rapt attention and lives the experience as it is being told. Our Lord and the Church have told us true stories concerning angels for several thousand years. We need to adopt this childlike simplicity that we may absorb the spirit of these ancient truths, accepting them as real.

Chapter XVIII

ISN'T IT DANGEROUS?

MANY will ask that question and rightly so. To seek mystical experience as an end in itself is the wrong objective. But in fearing the consequences of spiritual experience, which reaches out beyond the ordinary scope of the five senses, we are likely to limit ourselves in our development of a strong religion. We must realize that all vital forces are dangerous but to refuse to adventure because of risk is to paralyze spiritual growth. Electricity is dangerous, high voltage lines can cause fires and kill people, but we still use electrical power for every conceivable aid to human comfort. Occasionally, someone gets burned or loses his life, but that does not stop us from accepting the benefits that come to millions upon millions from the use of electricity. Just remember that everything which is powerfully good can also be powerfully dangerous if it is used for wrong motives and ends.

To seek an intimate association with loved ones who have left the flesh, if it be according to the will of God and for the purpose of mutual prayer and growth, is to practice the suggestions of the Book of Common Prayer. That means that we are approaching the subject with complete surrender to God's way of doing things and in the belief that in His great wisdom, which we cannot understand, He has seen fit to advance our departed to a new experience. It does not mean that we approach them with bitter frustrations, laments, and yearnings for their return to the old life in the flesh. Meister Eckhart, the great mystic of the middle ages, said that all frustrations are the result of seeking selfish ends rather than the will of God. So we approach communion with the departed with thanksgiving, with a humble heart, with a desire that God's will be done, and with the hope of as much of a sense of companionship and communion with them as God thinks best.

The one real danger that faces the person who seeks other-world communion is that which comes from visits to professional mediums. It would be unscientific indeed to deny the reality of some mediumistic communications for there is too much evidence spread over too many centuries merely to dismisss the cults with the condemnation that they are based only on superstition. Many serious-minded and scientific investigators have been greatly impressed by the various types of phenomena which they have seen or heard produced by people who appear gifted with powers of mediumship. Nor can we say that all people with these seeming gifts are cheap, insincere, and commercial, for there are individuals consecrated to the exploration of this fascinating field. Likewise, there are a rare few who seem to reach a high spiritual level, who are engaged in psychical and mystical research for unselfish reasons. These people should always receive a sympathetic ear from the Church. They should be heard and given sound counsel.

Yet, after full consideration of the whole movement of spiritualism, I would decidedly warn bereaved people against seeking solace through this dangerous avenue of approach. The Church has always been wise in her disapproval of the practice of spiritualism. I do not give warning because I deny the phenomenon, but, on the contrary, because I feel that much of it is almost too real and possibly evil. St. Paul warns us that our greatest enemy is not in the realm of the seen but of the unseen, for it is there that we must do battle against principalities and powers of spiritual wickedness emanating from high places. Too many modern psychological theologians have tried to explain away demoniac possession in psychiatric terms but such labels as "schizophrenia" and "manic depressive" still fail to explain the diabolical cleverness of evil possession. The Bible, the Church, and the Book of Common Prayer have long taught that such manifestations as big and little Hitlers are the results of intelligent and evil powers who inhabit and possess the human soul. It is quite possible that we may be so selfish in our yearning for our departed loved ones that, through the assistance of a medium, we cause them to associate with forces to which God never intended they be exposed in their new state of spiritual evolution. This is all quite speculative but worth the consideration of those who are tempted to seek communications by these means.

I know that when I was in grammar school, I played truant with a group of boys who had serious criminal records, facts I did not know at the time, and I came very close to possessing a court record of my own because, in a desire for adventure, I strayed from the school to which my parents had entrusted me.

The wise and loving Christian will not seek to satisfy his own yearning by striving to make contact with a loved one by a method which, since primitive times, has been closely associated with the mysteries of black magic. The Church is indeed a wise mother, and she has a technique by which we can be comforted and can receive a sense of spiritual communion with the departed in Paradise.

Some of the clergy are filled with concern because so many people are going to spiritualistic mediums and joining heretical and dangerous cults. They have good reason for such an attitude. They sometimes preach bitterly against it; they become caustic; they deplore the situation. The condemnation, however, should hardly begin with the medium, or the cult, or the seeker, but rather with the cleric who has not taught and practiced a concrete doctrine based on the teachings of the Church in the Book of Common Prayer. We have a liturgy built around the Holy Communion which is endless in its possibilities for comfort and interworld communion. Yet, for the most part,

Church people are quite ignorant of these opportunities. One must consider the consequences that may be met by the clergyman who neglects to instruct his people in the ways and teachings of the ancient lore of the Church as it pertains to the Communion of Saints and the presence of "Angels and Archangels, and the whole company of heaven" at the celebration of the Holy Communion. The greatest danger does not lie with the professional medium but with the priest or minister who, through neglect of his responsibility in teaching the faith in all its fullness, drives the bereaved to dangerous cults. Church leaders, see that you neglect not the doctrine of the Communion of Saints lest the bereaved stray in search of that which we possess but may have failed to present. See that frequent services of the Holy Communion are provided at varied hours so that the instructed bereaved may have ample opportunity to practice their faith in the Doctrine of the Communion of Saints.

Chapter XIX

TIME, SPACE, PRAYER

SUPPOSE the mother of a soldier who has died lives in Pittsburgh and his wife resides in Buffalo. Suppose both are going to a special service of the Holy Communion for him at the same time on the same day. We teach that he will be present with Christ at the Consecration in each place. How then can he be in Buffalo and Pittsburgh at the same moment?

I can point the way to an answer that helps satisfy me, although I am not able to enter into a scientific discussion of the time-space problem. Let it first be stated that many scientists now believe that both time and space are really one. Emmanuel Kant granted time a place of little importance in his thinking, stating that it was merely an aid to thought so that relative values might have some means of comparison and so be better understood. Some scholars interpret time in terms of space. It was the psalmist who said, "A thousand years in thy sight are but as yesterday." Living as we do at present, in a material world, it is practical to talk of time as measured by the clock, but everyone knows that the hour spent in loneliness by a GI on some South Pacific atoll seemed as years when compared to the hour spent on his last leave at home with his best girl.

When I used to broadcast every Monday night over the Mutual Network, I had stations in both Pittsburgh and Buffalo. I was just one person, broadcasting from one station into one microphone, yet, as an individual, I spoke in hundreds of homes in each city at the same time and, as a matter of fact, I did so over one hundred and ten stations. My voice was in any number of places at once due to the aid of radio waves. Certainly, if I can perform such an act, I have little trouble in believing that a soul in a spiritual body can do far greater and more mysterious things in the realm of the unseen.

If I were entirely consistent, I would not use such terms as "the other world" or "beyond" or "death," because I am resorting to the language of time and space, but unfortunately I don't know quite what to do about it when I, who inhabit a physical body, am here working a typewriter on earth.

A question often asked is, "In the next world will children who died long ago still be children, or will they be old men and women when we come in contact with them?" Certainly they do not grow old in terms of time for there is no time or age in the life eternal. The whole thing, the Bible would seem to intimate, will be a matter of growth of character and understanding and spiritual awareness.

The more we pray to get outside the physical world

while still on earth in order not to be bound by our time-space world, the easier it will be for us to comprehend the immensity of eternal life. Pray constantly for an expansion of your imagination, understanding, and vision, and the scope of life will take on vast new angles for you right here and now. You will start living in the Kingdom of Heaven while you still live in the Kingdoms of this world. "Thy kingdom come. Thy will be done, On earth as it is in heaven."

Remember our caterpillar who became a butterfly in the first chapter. While a caterpillar on the rug he lived in a limited time-space dimension, but when he became a butterfly, looking down at the rug, he saw where he had been yesterday, where he was today, and where he would be tomorrow. The past, present, and future were seen at one and the same time. The limits of the physical-present will be vastly changed in the spiritual-future.

Chapter XX

COMMUNICATION

MY SON and daughter are away at school. It is a new and lonely experience for Mrs. Pardue and me to live most of the year in a large house that is suddenly without their enthusiastic bursts of joy or temper. To say the least, we have been a bit lost without the life we have known for a good many years and in the silences that used to be delightfully interrupted by nobody knew what next. When our children were with us and had gone to bed, it was such an intimate experience to remain downstairs in the study and pray for them. I felt close to them because of the fact that, after all, they were in bed only a few feet away. Then, when they went away, they were many miles from us. It was not long before we accustomed ourselves, however, to the problem of separation by space because we had long believed that prayer knew no limitations. I can still remain in my study and, with practice, feel the miles melt between us as the unifying power of Christ makes us all one in Him. This takes time, thought, and trouble, and one can develop the experience only by believing it possible and practicing until one gets it. I can give you a few hints but you must do the work and the seeking. That, of course, is a basic spiritual law anyway; you must do the believing and the searching yourself.

So if I can pray for my boy and girl who are many miles away, and seen in the flesh but seldom, why can't I pray for the departed who are out of the flesh and not necessarily so many miles away? They, in their new plane of experience, are not living within the limits of time and space. Time, space, and material limitations are our particular impediments here on earth, for God has so organized this earthly school that these tough courses must be experienced. Now, the departed are free. What are the forces that can separate us from them? Lack of spiritual imagination and sin are those forces.

Sin is a separating force because sin weakens our relationship with Christ and only through His Divine Presence are we led into the Communion of Saints or communication with the departed. When we seek them through Him, we must enter into the relationship of interworld communication with an attitude of "Thy will be done" in our hearts. Thus, we do not seek them for any selfish reason, that we may tear them away from their work, from their new growth and assigned duties. We seek them for a moment of loving companionship or possibly for a bit of strengthening advice, for consultation with our Guardian Angels, because they, who know our problems so well, can see with a clarity such as we cannot comprehend. Indeed it is selfish to seek them when we are in a state of depression, yearning for them to be back. It certainly is contrary to the will and action of God, and it hardly makes our loved ones any happier to feel that we are carrying on here with so little faith. It may distract them from their new work and life. The sin of selfish yearning is really a case of self-indulgence which we are all likely to give in to for a while after a loved one's death. What undoubtedly does give those who have departed the joy of a healthy relationship is to know that we are carrying on faithfully and doing the best we know how; that we are seeking them for only a fleeting moment of loving companionship and courage; that this moment is reciprocal, for they help us as we help them by prayers and thoughts. Yet, the greatest companionship comes from mutual worship with them in the special mode provided by the service of the Holy Communion. If we are consistent in the faith, we must seek forgiveness and thus find strength in the joyous communion that is provided through the wisdom and practice of the Church.

Not only do we become separated from them by the sins of selfish yearning, but we are separated from them by unrepented sins which we have committed here in the world in which we live. All sin separates us from Christ; sins of lust, hate, lack of charity, egocentric domination, avarice, jealousy, selfishness, dishonesty, self-pity, and all the rest. Our loved ones may be right there at the Holy Communion where we are in attendance, but our unrepented sin is a separating element that seals us into a spirit-tight compartment making us immune to contact with them.

The other great separating force is lack of faith. "What things soever ye desire, when ye pray, believe that ye receive them and ye shall have them." Some people say that they have no faculty for praying with the imagination; that they are practical people who must have hard facts with which to deal. But, the cold, hard factualist is really just boasting for he uses his imagination every time he has a fear, or a worry. What are fears and worries but projections into the future with imagined facts that are as yet unsubstantiated on a basis of sound reasoning? We worry about sickness, poverty, inferiority, and a thousand and one other possibilities, but seldom do they come true. Are there any who do not worry or fear? Then he who has the capacity to worry and fear over purely imaginative and unfounded futures certainly can use his imagination to help his faith by basing it upon the fact of all the ages, namely, the life, death, and Resurrection of Jesus Christ and the millions of visible witnesses to that fact who compose the Christian Church.

In seeking spiritual union with them, you first use your faith by placing yourself in the presence of God. You may need to start at first with a picture, or a cross, or a crucifix, or whatever will make you feel near to Jesus, but you must start with Him to have right results. Then, through His presence, it is but a short step to theirs, for Paradise, their present abode, is where He promised to be in their company.

Chapter XXI

HIS AND THEIR REAL PRESENCE

NOW we come to the focal point of spiritual communication with the departed. It is centered in the traditional service of the Holy Communion. I believe we can aid them, and they us, at other times in prayer, but above all in the Sacrament of the Lord's Supper can we be closest to them, because we are then nearest to Him. When we talk about Christ's real presence in the Holy Communion, we do not mean "real" in the sense of "material." We hold with St. Paul that "the things which are seen are temporal, the things which are not seen are eternal." So, in the Holy Communion we refer to the real spiritual presence of our Lord in what has often been called "the Holy Mysteries."

Let us think a little further about the presence of Christ because everything thereon hinges. We must deny the general concept that God is *equally* present everywhere. But, He can be present where He wills to be. He can withdraw Himself when He so desires. He wills to be especially present at the Holy Communion, for thus did He declare Himself at the Last Supper. At this Feast He is always presiding at the head of the table and the elements of bread and wine are consecrated by Him through His

Church. By no means is this the only place where our Lord is present, for He is there when we offer so much as a cup of cold water to one who is in need. Likewise can He be with us in prayer and meditation. But sometimes these contacts have a sense of uncertainty about them, depending upon the individual's method and ability to approach God. The Holy Communion, however, is the only service that our Lord ever instituted Himself. It is there that He said He would especially be with us. It is not a matter of the worthiness of the priest, for no priest is worthy to celebrate the Holy Mysteries. "We are not worthy so much as to gather up the crumbs under thy table. But thou art the same Lord, whose property is always to have mercy." Our Lord is there in spite of human frailty, and is always present to give us His power in so far as we are prepared to receive it.

On the cross, our Lord answered the penitent thief's dying request to be remembered when He came into His Kingdom by saying, "Today, shalt thou be with me in Paradise." Paradise is a place of development, growth, and spiritual education (although we might better say that it is a state rather than a place). Since our Lord assures us that He will be with us in this period of development, we can be sure that the Christian departed are very close to the altar when He comes to us under the veiled mystery of bread and wine.

In the celebration of the Holy Communion, the prayer for the Whole State of Christ's Church makes it very clear that we are entering into a service which includes many more souls than those who are physically present. When we say "we and thy whole Church" we mean that those members of the Church now in Paradise are equally included in the office of "praise and thanksgiving." The moment we enter into this realm of "mystical union" distances disappear and many members of the unseen Church are united at this sacrament with "the glorious company of the Apostles, the goodly fellowship of the prophets, the noble army of martyrs, and the Holy Church throughout all the world."

Every time I attend the Holy Communion, I am with many friends whose physical bodies I have laid to rest or with those who were friends of mine when they were in the flesh. I was intimately associated with a number of boys in my parishes who were killed in the last war and are now with Him in Paradise. Among the many youngsters I have had the privilege of knowing in the Church, I can think of one especially who was with me at St. Paul's Cathedral, Buffalo. When I became Dean he was at Hobart College, an outstanding boxing champion. He was handsome, tough, whole-hearted, and spiritual. Earl Steiger was of a very unusual spiritual make-up and on Sundays during his vacations he was always in the sacristy ready to serve at the altar if we needed him. I had a number of talks with Earl about the matter of faith. The war came and he joined the Navy and became a fighter pilot on the carrier "Wasp." He was the first man from the "Wasp" to shoot down a four-motored Japanese bomber. It made him sick. After that he saw many of his own pals, as they descended in parachutes, strafed by Japanese pilots. From then on he didn't so much mind shooting down Japanese bombers. He was on the "Wasp" when she was sunk. He was in the water for many hours. He finally came back to Buffalo and looked me up. We talked together at length. When I asked him about his religion, he pulled a coin out of his pocket and touched the lettering underneath it with a strong thumb. It read "In God We Trust." On Sunday morning he was at the early Eucharist and back again at eleven. During that wonderful week, I married him to a splendid young girl who joined him in his religion. He went back into training and worked on the development of a new squadron. His new young wife was living near camp, and day after day he used to fly over the house dipping his wings. Then he went to sea again as the Chief Pilot of a baby carrier. In the most heroic way, he was killed making a final dive to put a Nazi submarine out of action. Earl and many others are at my altar time and again and join in worship when the celebrant says, "Therefore with Angels and Archangels, and with all the company of heaven, we laud and magnify thy glorious Name; evermore praising thee, and saying, Holy, Holy, Holy, Lord God of hosts, Heaven and earth are full of thy glory: Glory be to thee, O Lord Most High. Blessed is he that cometh in the name of the Lord, Hosanna in the Highest."

The Church could adopt no custom which would be more helpful in bringing spiritual reality to mourners than to have a celebration of the Holy Communion at the altar on the morning of a funeral, preceded by careful instruction. If the family is taught the meaning of the real presence of our Lord in the Sacrament, and the real fellowship of the departed with our Lord, there will be a background for the funeral service and for the future which will fortify the bereaved with the true meaning of the Resurrection. Furthermore, if the bereaved will go regularly to the Holy Communion with the knowledge that they can actually help the departed by prayer for their continual growth, the bereaved will have a religion of meaning and vitality. To make a habit, as Dr. Samuel Johnson did, of remembering your friends who have departed this life at the altar and of joining in their fellowship, is to begin to live in a world with a healthy reality tied up to eternity.

There is strong tradition that the Eucharistic relationship with the departed is reciprocal; that is, that our prayers are not always headed in one direction, namely, toward the help of the dead, but that our loved ones are likewise anxious to guide and help us. I frequently ask the assistance of good departed people, who, I am sure, see things with clearness and understand me and are capable of giving me sound advice on a spiritual basis.

I feel quite sure that my young friend, Earl Steiger, who so dearly loved the Church, assists me with his prayers and thoughts in my duties toward the returned service men. That does not mean that I have any right to shirk the responsibility of studying every possible angle of the problem of post-war adjustments, but it does mean that he gives me assistance in understanding things that can hardly come from academic study. The practical application has come through interviews and letters with dozens of service men. Dr. Samuel Johnson believed that aid might come from his departed wife. So he wrote this touching prayer in April 1752, "it being after twelve at night on the 25th."

"O Lord, Governor of Heaven and earth, in whose hands are embodied the departed spirits, if Thou hast ordained the souls of the dead to minister to the living, and appointed my departed wife to have care of me, grant that I may enjoy the good effects of her attention and ministrations, whether exercised by appearance, impulses, dreams, or in any other manner agreeable to Thy government; forgive my presumption, enlighten my ignorance, and however meaner agents are employed, grant me the blessed influences of Thy Holy Spirit, through Jesus Christ our Lord. Amen."

The late great Bishop C. H. Brent, Chaplain-in-Chief of the American Expeditionary Forces in the First World War, and the Apostle of Church Unity, was a man given to mystical experience and a strong believer in the Communion of Saints, particularly as it can be experienced at the Lord's Supper. He gave startling testimony pertain-

ing to the Communion of Saints in his little book called
Presence.* "Human presence is so completely volitional
that distance is no bar to its operation. My friends, whether
in the uttermost parts of the earth, or in Paradise, are with
me when I will them so to be. Time is as little a barrier as
space. Plato, Francis of Assisi, or Lincoln, come at my bid-
ding or beckoning. It is more than an act of memory that
brings them. There is no knowing how conscious such
fellowship or presence may become . . . The greater a
man is, the greater his power of presence. A world hero
like Buddha, or Livingston, is one whose presence is
universally available—not as an influence, but as a person; not as one who lived but as one who lives."

The Book of Common Prayer points to this mystical
union with another world. We have already made the
reference to "Angels and Archangels, and all the company
of heaven" wherein we are united with the unseen hosts
in praising God as we prepare for the consecration of the
bread and wine. It is well, however, to look at one of the
proper prefaces which further points to this union with
the departed. We call special attention to the proper preface for All Saints' Day, which says, "Who, in the multitude of thy Saints, hast compassed us about with so great
a cloud of witnesses that we, rejoicing in their fellowship,
may run with patience the race that is set before us, and,
together with them, may receive the crown of glory that
fadeth not away."

* Longmans, Green & Co. By permission.

This preface wonderfully sums up in one sentence the act of Eucharistic Communion with the departed. First it refers to the multitude of saints, which means all Christians and not just those who have been canonized by the Church. Secondly, it refers further to this great cloud of witnesses which surrounds us. In the third place, it reminds us that we should be filled with a sense of rejoicing because of our fellowship with them. And in the fourth place, asks that we may have patience in our remaining days here on earth so that we may receive the crown of glory with them.

The final paragraph in the prayer for the Whole State of Christ's Church is a great and hopeful statement, as well as a unifying force in bringing together the departed and the living—"And we also bless thy holy Name, for all thy servants departed this life in thy faith and fear; beseeching thee to grant them continual growth in thy love and service, and to give us grace so to follow their good examples, that with them we may be partakers of thy heavenly kingdom. Grant this, O Father, for Jesus Christ's sake, our only Mediator and Advocate."